BLESSINGS
IN THE
LIGHT
OF OUR
REDEMPTION

BLESSINGS
IN THE
LIGHT
OF OUR
REDEMPTION

Reza Safa

Harvesters World Outreach

Harvesters World Outreach
P.O. Box 2030
Camarillo, CA 93011
Phone: 805-445 7744
Web site: http://www.rezasafa.com

First printing, February 2012

CONTENTS

Dedicated

to

All the

Hungry

Souls of

Men and Women

Who Love

God, His

Truth, and

Are

Tired of Religion

ACKNOWLEDGEMENTS

I would like to thank my son, Jonathan, for his hard work on this book. You took the jumbled writings and untangled them. Your input is invaluable, son. I love you for who you are and what you have become, a man of God. I am proud of you.

Also, special thanks to Stacie Jennings for doing the final editorial work on this book. You have done a great job.

I would also like to thank my dear friend, Ben Ferrell of BMC Ferrell, for helping us get this glorious message of God's Redemption out to the masses through the mediums of television, and print.

Thank you all. I am grateful to the Lord for your labor of love on this book.

FOREWORD

N o subject is of more concern to the Body of Christ than that of tithing, giving, and blessings. Many churches err in this area and have caused great confusion among the people of God. Most teachings on this subject are based on the old covenant, which enforces the Law of Moses on the Body of Christ.

Constant teachings on money and forceful fundraising methods have left a dreadful impression of Christianity on unbelievers. As a result, the general consensus is that Christians are nothing more than a group of money-mongers and hypocrites. With such a reputation, it is no wonder we are loosing an entire generation of Americans. True Christianity is slowly but surely dying in a land that claims a great Christian heritage.

There is a misconception of the two covenants – both the old and the new. There remains an inability to rightly divide the word of truth in accordance to 2 Timothy 2:15: *Be diligent to present yourself approved to God, a worker who does not need to be ashamed, rightly dividing the word of truth.*

We do not differentiate what belongs to the old and new covenant. Our practices and teachings are based on a mixture of the two. People of God are perishing for lack of knowledge of the truth. Hosea 4:6

To know is to have strength.

The more we know, the stronger we are.
Knowledge is ability.
Knowledge protects us from error.
Knowledge is also freedom.
The more we know, the freer we are.

Today, a great part of the knowledge possessed by Christians is obtained through listening to common preachings – a common knowledge. The majority of born again Christians have minimal and basic knowledge of the Scripture.

These days, the most common preachings are merely inspirational. The preacher uses only a few scriptures during his sermon to encourage his battered congregation. With all due respect, the majority of church services of our day are no more than breadcrumb services – a lot of emotional hype with hardly any substance. The starving Church is falling into an abyss of obscurity, and she does not know it.

We do not need inspiration as much as we need information. As a matter of fact, preaching (*kerusso* in Greek) means proclaiming or heralding the Gospel. This kind of preaching is often associated with non-believers, the people outside of the church. Teaching (*didasko* in Greek), however, is to help believers learn, to disciple them. Teaching is for the Church.

This is where we are facing the problem. Preachers may inspire people to action without giving them a solid foundation in God's Word. It is like running in the sand; one has no strong footing.

For example, most preachers use the following verse to inspire and encourage their people to give money:

*Give, and it shall be given unto you; good measure, pressed down, and shaken together, and running over, **shall men give into your bosom.** For with the same measure that ye mete withal it shall be measured to you again.* Luke 6:38 KJV, Emphasis added

Well, this verse does sound like a good promise to get people to give money and reap a great harvest. But Luke 6:38 does not talk about money. If you read the entire passage, you will notice that it talks about how each individual should treat others – the way you treat others is the way you will be treated.

This principal may also be used for money, or whatever you may do for others. But notice, the promise is *men* will give back to you – not God.

This is not how Luke 6:38 is taught in today's churches. We are told if we sow money, God will give us back a greater measure.

If Luke 6:38 was about God returning the money, then Grace would loose its meaning. Notice the verse: *For with the same measure that you use, it will be measured back to you.*

If God were to give back to us in the same measure that we give, no one would be blessed or saved – simply because no one gives enough.

This book is about lifting the veil on our inheritance. It is about the truth of who we are and what we can do. The content will be new and challenging to many of you. Deep inside you may have known the truth about this matter, but somehow, for the respect of those in authority, you may have suppressed this truth. There is, however, an authority greater than any given name – God's eternal Word.

I encourage you to test what I write and to see whether it is in accordance with the truth of the Scripture. The truth is our only remedy in this hour, and we must protect it.

X

We are desperately in need of a true reformation in the Church. Many of today's practices and teachings in churches must go. They contradict the truth of God's Word and are harmful in nature. It does not matter who initiated these teachings and practices or how beneficial they have been. If they do not equate with the truth of the Gospel, they must be shunned.

I pray that this book may provoke you to think, study, and test all things in accordance with God's Word. Hopefully we will get out of the mess that religion has created, and heal all the mistrust and abuse in this area.

1

THE PRINCIPLE OF A COVENANT

To think correctly in regards to money, giving, and blessings, we must first have a better understanding of God's covenants.

God always operates within the framework of what He has promised – His covenants. The Bible speaks of several different covenants. There are, however, two covenants that relate to this subject matter and are of great importance to us. These two covenants are:

1. Old Testament (OT) or old covenant.
2. New Testament (NT) or new covenant.

In order for God to accomplish His will here on earth, He needs human beings. God is a spirit. Since spirit can only operate in the realm of the spirit, God needs flesh and blood through which He can operate in the physical realm. To do that, God goes into a binding contract with people. This is known as a *covenant*.

A covenant is an agreement that brings about a relationship of commitment between two parties. Once one agrees to the terms of the contract, he must be committed to it. It is a covenant of commitment.

God never breaks His covenant. When God cuts covenant with people, He will never ever breach that covenant. Regardless of what the other party does, He remains faithful to His covenant. People are unfaithful but faithfulness is an essential part of the divine nature. God cannot be unfaithful to His Word and His promises. 2 Timothy 2:13

Therefore know that the LORD your God, He is God, the faithful God who keeps covenant and mercy for a thousand generations with those who love Him and keep His commandments. Deuteronomy 7:9

God always operates according to His covenants. His dealings are only within the realm of His Word. Men operate outside of what they say and promise – God does not.

There are no amendments to God's constitution.

There is no reformation to the Law of God.

God does not err.

God cannot err. He knows the end from the beginning. God does not operate outside of His covenants. Furthermore, He does not mix one covenant with another.

God never mixes principles of the Old Testament (Law) with the New Testament (Grace) – never. This is of utmost importance for us to understand. This is the reason why we need to have a proper knowledge of the Old and the New Testaments.

Unfortunately many denominations, churches, and Christian leaders have mixed the principles of these two covenants. This has caused great confusion in the Body of Christ resulting in many unscriptural doctrines and practices, leaving many Christians disheartened and discouraged with the routine of church life.

The Frameworks of the Two Covenants

We can simply define the frameworks of the two covenants by the words of John the Apostle: *For the law was given through Moses, but grace and truth came through Jesus Christ.* John 1:17

The old covenant is based upon the Law of Moses, and the new covenant is based upon Grace.

In order to divide the Word of Truth and understand God's principle of both the Old and the New Testaments, we must divide the Bible into three major sections:

- Old Testament – Genesis to Malachi.
- The Four Gospels – Matthew, Mark, Luke, John.
- The Epistles –Acts through Revelation.

The Old Testament contains 39 books, 38 of which are dominated by the Law. Genesis is the only book not touched by the Law. It has many foundational truths concerning the origin of creation, the faith of Abraham, and the formation of the people and nation of Israel.

The four Gospels are still under the old covenant. This is where most people confuse the old and the new. Many believe that the four Gospels are within the framework of the new covenant because they are all about Jesus. This is where confusion begins.

The Four Gospels

The four Gospels are still legally under the old covenant. Actually, the new covenant did not take effect until Jesus rose from the dead and presented His

blood of the new covenant before the Father. Hebrews 9:12
During His life here on earth, Jesus was still
operating under the Law of Moses. The Bible says, *But
when the fullness of the time had come, God sent forth His
Son, born of a woman, born under the law, to redeem those
who were under the law, that we might receive the adoption
as sons.* Galatians 4:4-5

Jesus was born under the Law. He lived His entire
life under the Law of Moses. The transformation of the
old covenant into the new covenant began by Jesus'
death on the cross. The old covenant was still in full
operation until Jesus died on the cross and the veil of
the Temple was torn into two from top to bottom.

It is of utmost importance for us to understand that
the majority of Jesus' teachings, within the four
Gospels, relates to the Jews under the first covenant.
Pay close attention to the following scripture in the
book of Hebrews:

*And for this reason He is the Mediator of the new
covenant, by means of death…* Hebrews 9:15

This means the new covenant was not in effect until
Jesus died.

The new covenant needed Jesus' death.

His blood had to be shed before the new covenant
could take effect.

Jesus had to die in order for us to become
benefactors of the new covenant. We clearly see this in
the following verses:

*For where there is a testament, there must also of
necessity be the death of the testator. For a testament is in
force after men are dead, since it has no power at all while the
testator lives.* Hebrews 9:16-17

Notice what Paul is saying here: *A testament … has*

no power at all while the testator lives.

Look at verse 17 as it reads in the New International Version:

Because a will is in force only when somebody has died; it never takes effect while the one who made it is living.

We can boldly say that Jesus could not have taught the principles of the new covenant while He was still alive. He could not have done so because the new covenant had not started yet. He could not have taught the principles of the new covenant because no one was born again yet. The people, including His disciples, wouldn't have had the ability to understand or follow it.

Their spirit man was not yet regenerated.

They were still carnal beings – not spiritual.

One must be born again to understand the things of God's Spirit.

But the natural man does not receive the things of the Spirit of God, for they are foolishness to him; nor can he know them, because they are spiritually discerned. 1 Corinthians 2:14

Thus, the teachings of the new covenant could not be in effect during the lifetime of Jesus. This is an extremely important key in understanding the Bible and dividing the Word of Truth.

Jesus' Ministry to the Jews

Remember what Jesus said to the Canaanite woman in Matthew 15:24: *But He answered and said, "I was not sent except to the lost sheep of the house of Israel."*

Notice here, the Lord is saying that His earthly

ministry was aimed towards the Jews. If you study carefully, you will realize that the Lord Jesus ministered to only a few Gentiles, those outside of the Jewish people. His teachings were aimed at the Jewish people, those under the Law. He had to bridge between the old and the new covenants. He could not have taught the Gentiles because they had no covenant with God. He could not have taught the born again believers because there were none in His time.

He had not died yet.

He had not risen yet.

Sin was not put away yet.

His blood for the remission of sin was not shed yet.

So what Jesus taught, for the most part, was directed towards those under the Law of Moses. Many Bible teachers lack this knowledge.

Consequently, they teach what the Lord Jesus taught to the Jews, under the covering of the new covenant. They teach old covenant principles as the principles of the new covenant.

Now do not misunderstand me, Jesus taught many things that surpass old covenant bylaws. Teachings such as *the Nature of the Father, the Father's Personality, the Person and the Works of the Holy Spirit, His Relationship to the Father, Spiritual principles, etc.*, are not covenant related principles.

In regard to subjects that relate to the covenant of the Law, we must be careful not to teach them as principles of the new covenant or else we will contradict the Scripture. For instance, the Lord's Prayer,

In this manner, therefore, pray:
Our Father in heaven,
Hallowed be Your name.
Your kingdom come.
Your will be done
On earth as it is in heaven.
Give us this day our daily bread.
And forgive us our debts,
As we forgive our debtors.
And do not lead us into temptation,
But deliver us from the evil one.
For Yours is the kingdom and the power and the glory
forever. Amen. Matthew 6:9-13

Many churches and Christian denominations pray this prayer. This prayer was for the Jews under the old covenant. Notice how several points of the Lord's Prayer are fulfilled in Christ's Redemptive work. In verse 10 we are to pray for God's kingdom to come.

But His kingdom has come.

Remember when John preached saying, *the kingdom of God is at hand?* Mark 1:14-15

When Jesus began His ministry, God's kingdom began on the earth. Luke 11:20

The kingdom of God became a reality in us through Jesus' Death, Burial, and Resurrection. Prior to Jesus' death, God did not rule on the earth – satan did. John 14:30, 2 Corinthians 4:4

When Jesus died, satan's rule over mankind ended. Hebrews 2:14

Jesus put away sin. Hebrews 9:26

He destroyed the works of satan. 1 John 3:8

He took the keys of Hades and Death from him.

Revelation 1:18

Jesus triumphed over all the forces of darkness through His cross. Colossians 2:15

He became Lord and the Savior. Philippians 2:10-11

When one accepts Jesus as his Lord and Savior, He comes into that person's heart. This is God's kingdom on earth. It has come. Paul says, ...*for the kingdom of God is not eating and drinking, but righteousness and peace and joy in the Holy Spirit.* Romans 14:17

You see, the Kingdom of God is in those who have accepted the King of Glory.

Some may argue that the Lord's Prayer concerning *your kingdom come* is about the eternal kingdom of God. But this cannot be. The eternal kingdom of God will come whether we pray for it or not. When the contract that God has with mankind on the earth ends, His eternal kingdom will come.

Give us this day our daily bread.
He did.
He did make a provision.
...as His divine power has given to us all things that pertain to life and godliness, through the knowledge of Him who called us by glory and virtue... 2 Peter 1:3
He has blessed us.
Blessed be the God and Father of our Lord Jesus Christ, who has blessed us with every spiritual blessing in the heavenly places in Christ. Ephesians 1:3

Deliver us from evil.
He did.
He has delivered us from the power of darkness and conveyed us into the kingdom of the Son of His love...

Colossians 1:13

You are no longer under the dominion of satan.

You are no longer under the dominion of sin. Romans 6:14

He has delivered us through His Death, Burial, and Resurrection. Romans 4:24

Asking the Lord to deliver us again would be an insult. That would mean He has not delivered us yet.

If you had some ropes around your wrist and asked me to cut the ropes off, would you ask me again after I cut the ropes from your hands?

People repeat the Lord's Prayer in church every Sunday not knowing what they are saying. It is a religious repetition. They spit it out by memory.

Out of ignorance, they are insulting Jesus and His works.

Faith in God

Let me give you another example in regard to the Lord's teachings, in the four Gospels, based on the old covenant. Let us look at Mark 11:22-26:

So Jesus answered and said to them, "Have faith in God. For assuredly, I say to you, whoever says to this mountain, 'Be removed and be cast into the sea,' and does not doubt in his heart, but believes that those things he says will be done, he will have whatever he says. Therefore I say to you, whatever things you ask when you pray, believe that you receive them, and you will have them."

Notice in verse 22, Jesus commands the disciples to have faith in God or to have God's kind of faith.

Here, Jesus is specifically talking to His disciples who were Jews.

You must realize the ministry of the Lord Jesus to the Jews was mainly to prepare them for the coming kingdom. He had to get them out of the Law and prepare them for the coming of Grace. Jesus had to bridge the gap between the two covenants.

The distance between these two covenants is so vast that the natural man, under the old covenant, would have had a hard time crossing over into the new covenant. Jesus was helping the Jews to step across the gigantic gap that existed between the two covenants. I encourage you to get my book, *Two Covenants*, to have a better understanding of this subject.

For a Jew to believe in God, he had to see with his physical eyes. John 4:48 This is why God had to show the people of Israel all sorts of manifestations, types, and shadows.

Seeing and feeling are the only means by which the natural man can be led. In order to believe and obey God, the children of Israel had to have clouds covering them by day and pillars of fire by night as they went through the desert to the Promised Land. Even so, they still rebelled. The natural man cannot believe in something his senses do not register.

In Mark 11, Jesus is preparing the disciples for what is to come. He is preparing their hearts for a faith that could move mountains. He is making them hungry for what they will receive through His Redemption.

Mark 11:22 is not for a born again believer, the New Creation Man. According to the bylaws of the new covenant, we have faith.

What kind of faith?

We have God's kind of faith.

Look at 2 Peter 1:1: *Simon Peter, a bondservant and apostle of Jesus Christ, to those who have* **obtained like precious faith** *with us by the righteousness of our God and Savior Jesus Christ...* Emphasis added

You see here, Peter tells us that we have *received,* or obtained, the same kind of precious faith through the righteousness of our Lord Jesus Christ.

What kind of faith does God give?

Only God's kind – He would not give me man's kind of faith.

Man's type of faith does not please God. Hebrews 11:6

In the book of Romans, we are told that God has dealt a measure of faith to us. Romans 12:3

What kind of measure?

It must be God's measure.

It is the Father's measure. People argue about the words *a* or *the* before the word *measure.* Some say it should read *the measure of faith.* I agree, but really it does not matter because it is the Father's measure.

Have you seen a loving Father dealing out food to his children?

He gives them everything.

Most people I have heard talk on this subject speak as though God is the greediest Father – He portions out a little faith expecting you to increase it by reading the Scripture.

A thousand times **no**!

People misquote Romans 10:17, *So then faith comes by hearing and hearing by the word of God.*

This entire passage in Romans chapter 10 is about non-believers accepting the Lordship of Jesus.

The faith of God comes only through the hearing of God's Word. And that is what Romans 10:17 is saying.

According to 2 Peter 1:1, once a person believes in Christ, he has been given the faith of God. Therefore, Mark 11:20 is not for a believer. Jesus was talking to a Jew. When God gives, He gives *exceedingly abundantly.* Actually, He gives above all we can think or imagine. **Ephesians 3:20** Hallelujah.

So, we have faith.

We have God's measure of it.

And we have an abundance of it.

New Covenant Faith

Again in 2 Corinthians 4:13 Paul declares, *And since we have the same spirit of faith, according to what is written, "I believed and therefore I spoke," we also believe and therefore speak...*

You see, it would be unbiblical to tell a born again believer to have faith in God because he already has faith. It is like telling a mechanic to be a mechanic or a doctor to be a doctor. It simply does not make sense.

Every time a believer is told to have faith in God, he is being robbed of his faith. Now, one could encourage him to use what he has, but he should not be told to have it.

Instead, teach him how to use the faith he has been given by the righteousness of Jesus Christ.

When Jesus told His disciples to *have faith in God* in Mark 11:22, He could not have been talking to us; we have faith, the disciples did not. Their faith was a natural faith – the kind one must feel, hear, and sense in order to believe. Kenyon calls it *sense-knowledge* faith.

Yet, many preachers tell their church members that they need to believe God – that they need to have faith in God – instead of telling them about the faith that God has already given to them. They encourage their people to strive for something that is already theirs – a faith that has been obtained through the righteousness of our Lord and Savior.

Many of today's modern teachings are more of instructions than revelations of the truth. I like what Dr. T.L. Osborn, my personal friend and mentor, told me: "They teach ethics, social behavior." Their preachings are either sensational, which make you feel good about yourself, or instructional in social behavior – what to do and what not to do. They lack the revelation of who Jesus is and what He has accomplished for us in His Redemptive work.

Jesus' Teachings in the Four Gospels

There are many teachings of the Lord Jesus in the four Gospels that surpass covenant teachings or covenant bylaws. For instance, in verses 23 and 24 of Mark chapter 11, Jesus talks about the principles of God's kind of faith. God is a faith-God and the principles of faith surpass covenant bindings. Therefore, we can teach those same principles today as Jesus taught them in the four Gospels.

But notice Mark 11 verses 25 and 26. In verse 26 Jesus tells His disciples that if they do not forgive, they will not be forgiven.

And whenever you stand praying, if you have anything

*against anyone, forgive him that your Father in heaven may
also forgive you your trespasses. But if you do not forgive,
neither will your Father in heaven forgive your trespasses.*
Mark 11:25-26

Wait a minute – if my forgiveness depends upon
me forgiving others, then it is no longer Grace.

This is where we must understand with whom
Jesus was speaking. In this statement from Mark, Jesus
is speaking to the people under the Law – the Jews.

You may ask then, "What about Christians who do
not forgive others?"

Under the old covenant, God would hold back
forgiveness from such people because they broke the
Law. In the new covenant, it is all based upon the
finished work of Christ. It is God's Grace and our
response to that Grace, which is faith.

Grace made the provision for my forgiveness.

*In Him we have redemption through His blood, the
forgiveness of sins, according to the riches of His grace.*
Ephesians 1:7

Notice, it does not say *we will have forgiveness.*

It says *we have redemption through His blood, the
forgiveness of sins.*

We have it right now. How?

According to the riches of His grace.

Once you become a believer, all the provisions of
Christ's Redemptive work, whether forgiveness,
healing, restoration, or anything accomplished through
His Death, Burial, and Resurrection, will automatically
become yours.

All you need to do is believe in Him. John 6:29

It is not based upon what I do, but what He has

done.

Notice: *For by grace you have been saved through faith, and that not of yourselves; it is the gift of God.* Ephesians 2:8

Not of ourselves.

Do you see it?

This is the greatest truth of the new covenant ever made known to mankind.

A revelation of this truth will set man free. It will change anyone, no matter who they are or what they have done. This is what the Gospel is all about; it is the power of God unto salvation. Romans 1:16

Oh, that the church would grab a hold of this truth!

Works of Faith

One may ask, "What about our works?"

Do not misunderstand, I believe in works. But I believe in the works of faith – the works that proceed after the new birth experience.

The new creation in us will lead us to forgive.

It is unnatural for a Christian to walk in unforgiveness. Love automatically becomes our attitude as a result of God's nature in us through the new birth.

The Bible tells us, ...*the love of God has been poured out in our hearts by the Holy Spirit...* Romans 5:5

It goes against the grain of a born again Christian to walk in unforgiveness. His heart, or his spirit man, will condemn him. 1 John 3:20

If a Christian does not listen to the voice of his own spirit and continues in his error, he will lose fellowship and confidence with the Father. He will miss out on

God's blessings; not because the Father withheld them from him, but because of his broken fellowship with the Father.

Notice what Paul says to the believers in Ephesus regarding forgiveness: *And be kind to one another, tenderhearted, forgiving one another, even as God in Christ forgave you.* Ephesians 4:32

Notice the tense, *forgave you.* It is in the past tense. It is done.

It does not say if you do not forgive, you will not be forgiven.

Any time we see an *if* before a command in the Scripture, it means the command is conditional. If we meet the condition, then God will meet us with the blessings of that command. This is the framework of the old covenant.

Under the old covenant, people were not born again.

Their spirits were not one with God's Spirit.

They did not have the Spirit of God in them.

The Holy Spirit of God came upon certain people, for a short period of time, when they were called to a certain task.

God's Spirit did not dwell in them permanently.

Usually we read the phrase, "The hand of God came upon him," or "The Spirit of the Lord came upon him."

The Law of God was not written in their hearts.

So in order for God to make them to obey Him, He had to put conditions to His commandments such as: "If you do this, I will do that for you," or "If you take heed and obey my commandments, then I will cause these blessings to come upon you." Deuteronomy 28:1-2

If you are willing and obedient, you shall eat the good of the land. Isaiah 1:19

A "Jesus Plus Plan"?

Under the old covenant, blessings were conditional.
People of God had to be willing and obedient.
Forgiveness was conditional.
Healing was conditional.
They had to give gifts when they were healed.
They had to give in order to receive.
They had to forgive in order to be forgiven.

The moment Jesus rose from the dead and stood before God's presence on our behalf, we were given all of heaven's blessings. *Blessed be the God and Father of our Lord Jesus Christ, who has blessed us with every spiritual blessing in the heavenly places in Christ.* Ephesians 1:3

Before I did anything to earn a single blessing, He secured it for me by His Grace.

There is absolutely nothing I can do to earn God's blessings.

Nothing.

Our righteousness does not equate to God's level of righteousness at any time or at any rate, no matter how much good we do. It is like an ordinary first grader who tries to compete with Einstein in mathematics.

Impossible.

Our righteousness and His righteousness are in two separate realms that cannot be connected by any means.

No matter what we do, we cannot earn the favor of

God or His blessing.

It is only through Grace that we receive anything from Him.

It is not our doing, but all His doing.

Notice again Ephesians 4:32: *...even as God in Christ forgave you.*

When did He forgive us?

When Jesus paid the penalty for our sins.

His Grace forgave us.

His Love forgave us.

Grace is simply God's Love in action – God's Love making the provision for us.

Ephesians 1:3 was secured and sealed for us before we were born.

God blessed us before we gave a dime to Him.

All anyone needs to do to possess all of God's blessings is to simply believe in Jesus and what He has done in His Death, Burial, and Resurrection.

That is all.

Jesus summarizes this amazing truth in John 6:28-29: *Then they said to Him, "What shall we do, that we may work the works of God?" Jesus answered and said to them, "This is the work of God, that you believe in Him whom He sent."*

In other words, this is all God is asking you to do: *Believe in Jesus.*

Faith is based upon a finished work.

It is finished. It is done.

Just believe in a done deal.

Just believe in His finished work.

Forgiveness is done. Ephesians 1:7

Healing is done. 1 Peter 2:24

Salvation is done. Hebrews 9:12
Blessings are done. Ephesians 1:3
Faith is done. 2 Peter 1:1
Even faith is provided for us. Just take it. Romans 12:3
Take all His goodness. John 1:16
Take all His Love. It is all free. Romans 8:32

Most of the teachings we hear on faith, healing, giving, forgiveness, and deliverance are based upon the Law, the old covenant. It is Jesus' works, plus mine.

If I were to give, *then* He would bless me!

If I were to believe Him for healing, *then* He would heal me!

If I were to forgive others, *then* He would forgive me!

In other words, it is my *works* that bring the reality of Jesus' Redemption into my life. Not my faith, but my works!

I call it, **"The Redemption Plus Plan."** It is the work of Jesus PLUS mine.

A **"Jesus Plus Plan."**

SOWING A SEED?

F or the past thirty years or so, a new concept has
been developed among the Pentecostal and
Charismatic churches throughout the world – the
concept of sowing and reaping.

It is taught that if we give money, we will reap
more in return. Various scriptures from both the Old
and the New Testaments have been used to prove this
point.

The concept of financial sowing and reaping is used
as a fund-raising method to encourage people to give
money to the work of the Lord. Recently, however, it
has become more of a doctrinal principle due to its
widespread and exaggerated emphasis. It is a
stumbling block to millions of people worldwide, both
Christians and non-Christians. Since it is causing more
harm than good, we must deal with it from a biblical
standpoint.

Is the idea of sowing and reaping, in regards to
finances, a biblical concept?

Sowing & Reaping

God placed a law in nature that would cause the earth

to bring forth seeds, which would then multiply themselves. In the book of Genesis we read:

Then God said, "Let the earth bring forth grass, the herb that yields seed, and the fruit tree that yields fruit according to its kind, whose seed is in itself, on the earth"; and it was so. And the earth brought forth grass, the herb that yields seed according to its kind, and the tree that yields fruit, whose seed is in itself according to its kind. And God saw that it was good.

And God said, "See, I have given you every herb that yields seed which is on the face of all the earth, and every tree whose fruit yields seed; to you it shall be for food." Genesis 1:11-12, 29

Also in Genesis 8 we read:

While the earth remains, seedtime and harvest, cold and heat, winter and summer, and day and night shall not cease. Genesis 8:22

These and other scriptures from the New Testament are used to prove the idea of financial sowing and reaping:

Do not be deceived, God is not mocked; for whatever a man sows, that he will also reap. Galatians 6:7

If you study every scripture used to connect finances into the law of sowing and reaping, you will notice that they are all taken out of context.

Sowing and giving are two different concepts.

Sowing seed and giving money (tithes, offerings, and gifts) are two completely different principles. One cannot give money to a needed cause and expect that money to be returned to him multiplied.

Some even use the parable in Mark chapter four, where the Lord Jesus taught the condition of man's heart, to say that the returns on their giving would be thirty-fold, sixty-fold, or one hundred-fold.

Money, A Seed?

Giving and sowing are two different concepts. One cannot mix these two concepts and expect the same result.

You cannot give an apple to someone and expect thirty, sixty, or one hundred apples in return. Now, if you were to sow an apple seed into the ground, after many years the ground would yield an apple tree. From this tree you may harvest thirty, sixty, or one hundred apples.

In like manner, you cannot give money away and expect it to be returned to you multiplied. If you were to take your money, however, and invest it wisely, then you may get a thirty, sixty, or one hundred-fold return.

If what they are saying is true, then every Christian who has ever given money would be extremely wealthy.

The United States of America gives billions of dollars in grants every year to various third world nations. Yet, the United States is up to her neck in trillions of dollars of debt.

To justify the promised return, they say that one must *believe* when one gives – "sow into a good ground." Thus, they are mixing the concept of the Law (*if* you give) with the concept of Grace (faith). This teaching in and of itself is contradictory.

The Law does not need faith. Galatians 3:12

Grace, however, does. Romans 5:2

How can one keep the Law and believe for its

manifestation at the same time? It is like believing that when I maintain the speed limit, the policeman will not give me a ticket. What? Of course he will not give me a ticket if I am going the speed limit.

Yet, in churches, we are told to believe God for a great return on our giving! There is even a new saying, *If you do not expect back a return on your giving, you have not given properly!* And then, they quote Luke 6:38. Wow!

Giving & Sowing

Giving relates to the attitude of the heart, while sowing is a matter of being diligent in our labor. If we mix these two concepts, we will develop an attitude of laziness – a mentality which believes in getting things easily, such as debt cancellation, debt forgiveness, money multiplication through giving, promotion without hard work, favor, open doors, and on and on.

This kind of teaching will produce in us an ineffective spirit. We will become unproductive. I believe this is what is happening in the modern church today. People want an easy way out, and they call it faith. We are giving birth to a generation of men and women who expect things without working hard for it.

It is one thing to believe God's promises and blessings, yet it is another to desire things to be handed to us. The Scripture commands us, *If anyone will not work, neither shall he eat.* 2 Thessalonians 3:10

This idea of giving in order to get back is not in accordance with God's loving nature. It is the nature of greed and selfishness. I become the subject matter.

To give is to love.

If you expect to receive back what you have given, you have not loved.

An investment in a company does not necessarily mean you love that company. You bought shares and rightfully expect a return on your investment. Some folks will take legal action against a company that did not fulfill what was promised to them.

Could this be why so many Christians these days are mad at God?

A true act of giving has no other motive than love itself.

If you expect to get back what you have given, you have not truly given.

The very fact that you have given means that you do not expect back. We call it an offering, donation, or sacrifice.

"But what about Luke 6:38," one may ask?

Luke 6:38

In regard to giving, we have been reminded time and time again of Luke 6:38 – If we give, *it will be given to us good measure, pressed down, shaken together, and running over.*

Let's take a closer look at this passage in the Gospel of Luke:

Judge not, and you shall not be judged. Condemn not, and you shall not be condemned. Forgive, and you will be forgiven.

Give, and it will be given to you: good measure, pressed down, shaken together, and running over will be put into your bosom. For with the same measure that you use, it will be measured back to you. Luke 6:37-38

First and foremost, this passage does not talk about money. Read the whole passage and you will understand that Jesus is referring to how we should treat one another.

For the sake of argument, let's say it is about money. Even so, notice that Luke 6:38 does not talk about how God gives into your bosom; rather, people do. The King James Translation of verse 38 reads:

*Give, and it shall be given unto you; good measure, pressed down, and shaken together, and running over, **shall men give into your bosom**. For with the same measure that ye mete withal it shall be measured to you again.* Emphasis added

Notice: *Shall **men** give into your bosom.*

Also pay attention: *For with **the same measure** that ye mete withal it shall be measured to you again.* People will give back with the same measure – not thirty, sixty, or hundred-fold measures as it is believed.

The adjectives **we use** for our measuring cup should be, *"good measure," "pressed down," "shaken together,"* and *"running over."* It cannot be the other way around.

But this is not what many churches teach today. They say if we give, **God** will give back to us good measure, pressed down, shaken together, and running over. They have twisted this verse completely.

It is a very simple principle – when you give and are generous towards others, your generosity will have an impact on them and they, in return, will be generous towards you.

God's Blessings

Under the new covenant, we can earn absolutely nothing from God. I mean nothing.

Everything we have is because of what Jesus has done. Everything we receive from God is because of what Jesus has accomplished in His Redemptive work. There is not a single blessing under the new covenant that I have *earned* – not one.

Notice what the Scripture declares: *Blessed be the God and Father of our Lord Jesus Christ, who has blessed us with every spiritual blessing in the heavenly places in Christ…* Ephesians 1:3

You see, God blessed me with *every spiritual blessing.* The King James translation says, *all spiritual blessings.*

When did He bless you with *all spiritual blessings*?

Was it when you gave a $50 gift to a ministry?

Was it when you paid your tithe?

Yes? No?

When did He bless you, then?

Verse four tells us when:

… Just as He chose us in him before the foundation of the world, that we should be holy and without blame before him in love… Ephesians 1:4

He blessed us when He chose us in Him before the foundation of the world. What does this mean?

Grace – the divine Love in action.

Hallelujah.

I was blessed in Christ before I gave a dime to Him. Notice the following Scripture:

For you know the grace of our Lord Jesus Christ, that though He was rich, yet for your sakes He became poor, that you through His poverty might become rich. 2 Corinthians 8:9

He became poor so that you and I can be rich (fully supplied).

Notice: *You through His poverty might become rich.*

Not through my giving, **but through His poverty.**

The word *rich* here means *fully supplied.* God made a full supply for us through what Jesus did, not what I did or can do.

Do not let this truth pass you by easily. Go over it again.

You see, if our blessings were dependent upon our giving, then Jesus died and became poor in vain. Plus, I would have had a cause to boast of my generosity before God. But I cannot brag before God. The Bible says:

For by grace you have been saved through faith, and that not of yourselves; it is the gift of God, not of works, lest anyone should boast. Ephesians 2:8-9

Notice, it is *not of works.*

It is not my giving.

It is not my generosity.

It is not my good heart.

It is ALL Him.

That is what His Grace is all about – we have what we have because of what He gave, not because of what we gave.

Look at what Paul says in Romans 8:32: *He who did not spare His own Son, but delivered Him up for us all, how shall He not with Him also freely give us all things?*

Pay attention to the word *freely* in this verse: *...shall He not with Him also **freely** give us all things?*

Freely means I did not do anything for it. It is free. It is a gift.

You do not do anything to receive a gift. Did you give people money before they gave you a birthday present?

It is His Grace making it possible. It is His Love.

Grace Made All Provision

Under the bylaws of the new covenant, God does everything through Jesus. That is the format of Grace.

Everything in the new covenant is connected to what Jesus has accomplished through His Death, Burial, and Resurrection. Even when God uses us, it is as a result of what Jesus has done. So when I do something for God, it is His Grace in me that causes me to do the work.

Notice what Paul says concerning this amazing truth: *But by the grace of God I am what I am, and His grace toward me was not in vain; but I labored more abundantly than they all, yet not I, but the grace of God which was with me.* 1 Corinthians 15:10

Here, Paul is comparing himself with the other apostles.

He says that *he labored more abundantly than they all.* Well, if it is his work, then he could boast of his piety before God. But notice: *…yet not I, but the grace of God which was with me.*

Do you see it?

Let's take a look at this concept in regard to giving. If you are a giver and you give generously, it is simply because of His Grace in you. The difference between you and other greedy Christians is that you have responded to the Grace of God, they did not.

The Bible says, *And God is able to make all grace abound toward you, that you, always having all sufficiency in all things, may have an abundance for every good work.*
2 Corinthians 9:8

It is His Grace making the provision for you to abound and have abundance for every good work. The burden has been taken off of you, and been laid on Him.

Thus, no one can have an excuse for not *giving*, or boast for their *giving*.

The question may arise, "Why then should I give?"

If you ask the above question, it is because you have been wrongfully taught. You gave because you wanted to get back. You made a deal with God. You gave because the preacher forced you to give. You operated under the Law. You bought your blessings from Him. You exchanged your money for His Grace.

Why should we give?

We give because we love Him who gave Himself for us.

We give because He said *give*.

We give because He first gave.

We give because we love the Gospel.

We give because giving is a part of our new nature – the Love nature.

Love gives.

Love makes sacrifices.

We give simply because His nature is in us.

What about tithing? Shall we tithe?

Let's study this subject in the Scripture.

TITHE OR TITHING

There is not a more perplexing subject discussed among the believers than the subject of tithing. There is a lot of confusion in the area of tithing. Are the following questions familiar to you?

Do I tithe before taxes or after?

Do I tithe on net or gross?

Can I give a portion of my tithe to the needy?

Can I give a portion of my tithe to my family?

Do I tithe on gifts?

We need to study this subject carefully and see what is commonly being taught in churches today, and what is in accordance with the new covenant.

Tithing in the Old Testament

First of all, the word *tithe* means ten percent. Abraham was the first person of whom we have a record of paying tithe in the Old Testament. We read in Genesis:

Then Melchizedek king of Salem brought out bread and wine; he was the priest of God Most High. And he blessed him and said: "Blessed be Abram of God Most High, possessor of heaven and earth; And blessed be God Most

High, Who has delivered your enemies into your hand." And he gave him a tithe of all. Genesis 14:18-20

Here, Abraham returns from a victorious battle with certain kings. Out of the spoils that he captured, he gave tithe to Melchizedek, the priest of the Most High God.

We have no record of Melchizedek in regard to his background and how he became a high priest of God. At that time, there were no written laws or ordinances of God. Any known revelation of God was based on the personal experiences of each individual with Jehovah God.

The question is, how did Abraham know to give tithe? Had God revealed it to him? We do not know the answer. Nowhere in the Scripture are we told anything concerning the revelation of tithe to Abraham. It could not have been required of Him as a law since the Law was given some four hundred years later. So why did Abraham give tithe?

We read in the book of Hebrews 7:1-10, *For this Melchizedek, king of Salem, priest of the Most High God, who met Abraham returning from the slaughter of the kings and blessed him, to whom also Abraham gave a tenth part of all, first being translated "king of righteousness," and then also king of Salem, meaning "king of peace," without father, without mother, without genealogy, having neither beginning of days nor end of life, but made like the Son of God, remains a priest continually. Now consider how great this man was, to whom even the patriarch Abraham gave a tenth of the spoils. And indeed those who are of the sons of Levi, who receive the priesthood, have a commandment to receive tithes from the people according to the law, that is, from their brethren, though they have come from the loins of Abraham; but he whose genealogy is not derived from them received tithes from Abraham and blessed him who had the promises. Now beyond all contradiction the lesser is blessed by the better. Here mortal men receive tithes, but there he receives them, of whom it is witnessed that he lives. Even Levi, who receives tithes, paid tithes through Abraham, so to speak, for he was still in the loins of his father when Melchizedek met him.*

Notice verse 8: *Here mortal men receive tithes, but there he receives them, of whom it is witnessed that **he lives.*** Emphasis added

Melchizedek was a type of Christ. When Abraham gave tithe to Melchizedek, he actually gave tithe to Christ. The question is, for what reason?

It is interesting to note that Abraham did not give tithe prior to meeting Melchizedek. This means tithe was for a specific goal.

Somehow Abraham had a revelation of supporting God's priest. This could have been the custom of his day, that people supported priests of their own religions. Thus, Abraham followed what was a common principle. Then again, there is no scripture supporting any theory as to why Abraham gave tithe.

What is interesting is that Abraham gave ten percent. Where did he get the idea of ten percent? Why not five percent or fifteen percent?

It is also important to observe that although Abraham was not under the Law, he was neither a born again believer nor a New Creation Man.

Tithing According to the Law

When the Law of Moses was established, God needed officers or priests of the Law. God gave this task to the Levites, the children of Aaron. To support Levites, God ordained tithing – **ten percent of everything a Jew would earn, make, or grow.**

We read in Leviticus 27:30-34, *And all the tithe of the land, whether of the seed of the land or of the fruit of the tree, is the LORD's. It is holy to the LORD. If a man wants at all to redeem any of his tithes, he shall add one-fifth to it. And concerning the tithe of the herd or the flock, of whatever passes under the rod, the tenth one shall be holy to the LORD. He shall not inquire whether it is good or bad, nor shall he exchange it; and if he exchanges it at all, then both it and the one exchanged for it shall be holy; it shall not be redeemed. These are the commandments which the LORD commanded Moses for the children of Israel on Mount Sinai.*

Ten percent of Israel's income was to be given to the Levites. They in turn would tithe to the Aaronic priests. Numbers 18:21-28

Tithing, according to the Law of Moses, had three objectives:

1) To support the Priests and the Levites. Numbers 18:21

2) To sponsor communal meals. Worshippers, together with their families, were to consume a portion of their tithe before the Lord at the Temple. Deuteronomy 14:23-26

3) To support the fatherless, aliens, and widows who dwelt in the land of Israel. Deuteronomy 14:28-29

When children of Israel neglected to give their tithes, the Levites and the priests suffered. Consequently, the Temple and the worship of Jehovah

God suffered lack. We see this clearly in the time of Nehemiah. Nehemiah 13:4-13

Right after the conquest of Babylon by the Persians, God raised several great men to lead the children of Israel back to their homeland. These men were to restore the city of Jerusalem, the Temple, and the ordinances of Jehovah God. These men were Ezra, Zerubbabel, Nehemiah, and a few other minor prophets.

Nehemiah was burdened to restore the torn down walls of Jerusalem and the Temple of God, which was in ruins. After his return to the land of Israel, he realized that the worship of Jehovah God was neglected, the House of God was in rubble, and the Levites and priests had gone back to their fields for they had no support.

I also realized that the portions for the Levites had not been given them; for each of the Levites and the singers who did the work had gone back to his field. So I contended with the rulers, and said, "Why is the house of God forsaken?" And I gathered them together and set them in their place. Then all Judah brought the tithe of the grain and the new wine and the oil to the storehouse. And I appointed as treasurers over the storehouse Shelemiah the priest and Zadok the scribe, and of the Levites, Pedaiah; and next to them was Hanan the son of Zaccur, the son of Mattaniah; for they were considered faithful, and their task was to distribute to their brethren. Nehemiah 13:10-13

During this time, the prophet Malachi warns the people concerning their apathy and disregard for the worship of Jehovah God. Malachi, in his book, addresses a series of rebukes and encouragements, trying to restore the people's covenant with the God of Israel.

In the third chapter of his book, well known to today's preachers and church folk, Malachi rebukes the people for defrauding the Lord by withholding the required tithes and offerings. He warns them of the consequences of their action.

"For I am the LORD, I do not change;
Therefore you are not consumed, O sons of Jacob.
Yet from the days of your fathers
You have gone away from My ordinances
And have not kept them.
Return to Me, and I will return to you,"
Says the LORD of hosts.
"But you said,
'In what way shall we return?'
"Will a man rob God?
Yet you have robbed Me!
But you say,
'In what way have we robbed You?'
In tithes and offerings.
You are cursed with a curse,
For you have robbed Me,
Even this whole nation.
Bring all the tithes into the storehouse,
That there may be food in My house,
And try Me now in this,"
Says the LORD of hosts,
"If I will not open for you the windows of heaven
And pour out for you such blessing
That there will not be room enough to receive it.
"And I will rebuke the devourer for your sakes,
So that he will not destroy the fruit of your ground,
Nor shall the vine fail to bear fruit for you in the field,"

Says the LORD of hosts;
"And all nations will call you blessed,
For you will be a delightful land,"
Says the LORD of hosts. **Malachi 3:6-12**

Notice verse 9: *You are cursed with a curse, for you have robbed Me, even this whole nation.*

God told them that they were robbing Him! Why? The tithe belonged to God. It belonged to His Temple. It was for His service. It was a part of the covenant He had with Israel. Naturally, there were consequences when the Laws of that covenant were broken.

Are Christians Cursed?

Every Sunday, all around the world, many preachers and pastors use the same scriptures from Malachi that were specifically given to Israel, telling their people that they are under a curse because they do not tithe.

It is said that only 3% to 6% of all Christians tithe. If what these preachers are saying is true, then 94% to 97% of all Christians are cursed with the curse of the Law. **Deuteronomy 28**

This means the Body of Christ has, for the past 2000 years, been operating under the curse of the Law.

Is this really true?

You mean to say, Christianity has been under this curse for the past two thousand years and Jesus never set us free from the curse of the Law?

I guess Galatians 3:13 is not true then, since Jesus did not *redeem us from the curse of the Law* after all.

Christ has redeemed us from the curse of the law, having

become a curse for us for it is written, "Cursed is everyone who hangs on a tree." Galatians 3:13

To justify the above scripture, this argument is brought forth: Since tithing was before the Law, tithing surpasses the Law. Thus, people are under the curse because they do not tithe.

Now, I want you to realize how contradictory this theory is. Pay attention, the above verse states that we have been redeemed *from the curse of the law.* This means the curse is related to the Law, if it is *the curse of the law.*

There could not have been a curse before the Law because the Scripture says, *For until the law sin was in the world, but sin is not imputed when there is no law.* Romans 5:13

Go over this verse again and notice that *sin is not imputed when there is no law.*

For example, if you break the speed limit in a 25 mph zone, you will get a ticket. But where there is no speed limit sign you cannot be ticketed if you drive 35 mph.

So, *the curse of the law* could not have existed before the Law.

Therefore, Galatians 3:13 does relate to the Law of Moses.

If Jesus redeemed us from that curse, then we cannot be under it any longer. Can we?

You have to get this, or religion will confuse you with all kinds of philosophies and it will eventually condemn you.

So now we ask, "Is tithing for today?"

Is Tithing An Everlasting Ordinance?

If tithing were an everlasting ordinance that surpassed the Law of Moses, then Paul would have definitely taught about it in his Epistles.

In regard to giving money to the church and the needs of the house of God, Paul taught two whole chapters: 2 Corinthians 8 and 9.

Paul does not mention tithing a single time in these two chapters or in any other of his Epistles – not once. The only place in the Epistles where we see the word tithe being mentioned is in Hebrews chapter 7, which we mentioned earlier. Again, it was in regard to Abraham and Melchizedek.

Tithing takes away the principle of sonship.

Tithing belongs to servants and those who are not members of the household of God.

Tithing is an ordinance for a servant.

It was all that God could get out of a man who is not born again.

In regard to giving, David was the only one, in the Old Testament, who operated beyond the covenant bindings.

David actually acted more like a son than any other Bible personality under the old covenant. Read chapters 28 and 29 of 1 Chronicles and you will understand what I mean.

Notice the following verses in chapter 29:14, 16:

But who am I, and who are my people, that we should be able to offer so willingly as this? For all things come from You, and of Your own we have given You.

"O LORD our God, all this abundance that we have prepared to build You a house for Your holy name is from

Your hand, and is all Your own." Emphasis added

Somehow David's relationship with God surpassed the Law. He did not fit well under the Law. He acted as a son, although he never experienced the new birth. I think it is because of David's heart for God that caused him to give like he did. He was not required, according to the Law, to give in this manner. He gave over one trillion dollars in offerings for the building of the Temple in Jerusalem. What was it? He was in love with God. He acted as a son.

The Law Limits Sons

Sons cannot fit under the Law of Moses.

The Law condemns sons.

The Law binds a son and prohibits him from operating in the fullness of his relationship with the Father. This is evident in the way the Lord Jesus broke, on several occasions, the rules of Sabbath. In one instance, He healed a man with a withered hand on the Sabbath. Luke 6:6-11

The so-called keepers of the Law plotted against His life because He had healed someone on the Sabbath.

Jesus broke the Sabbath. Why?

To heal someone.

Of course, that religious bunch did not realize the Sabbath was given for our sakes, for us to rest – not vice versa. Plus, Jesus was the Lord of the Sabbath. He instituted it. He was the Sabbath Himself. He is our rest.

The Law brings condemnation.

The Law is a ministry to condemn people. It is known as the ministry of condemnation. 2 Corinthians 3:9

The Law is called the ministry of death. 2 Corinthians 3:7

The letter kills. 2 Corinthians 3:6

Every time a preacher speaks on tithing, he condemns his people.

Every time a pastor teaches his people from Malachi 3:10, he robs people of their generous spirit. He is actually telling his people that they are bad givers. This is what the Law was for.

The Law was not given to make people generous, but for people to realize they do not give as they should.

Therefore by the deeds of the law no flesh will be justified in His sight, for by the law is the knowledge of sin. Romans 3:20

Yet, many use the Law to force people into a higher level of giving.

That is foolishness!

The Law does not have such capability. If it did, we would have no need for Jesus.

You have to get this. This is a paramount truth that will set Christianity free and set it on fire for God.

Every preacher that preaches on tithing condemns his people and hinders them from giving. He actually binds the spirit of sonship – a generous spirit in God's children.

The Jewish people were under the curse because they broke the Law of God. Notice the following verse:

For as many as are of the works of the law are under the curse; for it is written, "Cursed is everyone who does not continue in all things which are written in the book of the law, to do them." Galatians 3:10

Paul is talking about the Jews who persisted in following the Law.

Israel has been ruled and subjected by almost every force known to man. The only time Israel had an era of blessing and victory was during the reign of David. Even so, David caused several major curses to come upon God's covenant people. You need to study the time of David in the Old Testament.

Even today, Israel, with all its military might, has not experienced a time of peace since its statehood. Isn't that amazing?

Do you know of any other people group that has suffered as much as the Jews? If it were not because of God's unconditional covenant with Abraham, very few Jews would be alive today.

I love Israel, both the nation and her people. I have a great burden for them to know the truth. Please read my book, *Two Covenants, Three People,* so that you may understand this very important teaching.

We need to pray for Israel and the peace of Jerusalem; that the eyes of their understanding may be enlightened, and that they may be delivered from the bondage of the Law.

When preachers enforce any Law of Moses, including tithing, they enslave God's people back into the bondage of the Law. They literally bring curses upon their people. They bind and condemn God's people who are purchased freely by the Blood of God's Lamb.

Notice what Paul tells the churches of Galatia:

For as many as are of the works of the law are under the curse; for it is written, "Cursed is everyone who does not continue in all things which are written in the book of the law, to do them." Galatians 3:10

Not only are they under the curse, but they have also fallen from Grace.

Christ is become of no effect unto you, whosoever of you are justified by the law; ye are fallen from grace. Galatians 5:4 KJV

This means if you trust that you will be blessed through your giving, Jesus' works will have no effect in your life. It means His Grace is ineffective in the area of your life where you lean on your own works.

This is a serious matter.

I believe this is the reason why many churches, which preach on tithing, are struggling financially.

The Spirit of A Son

The spirit that God has put in a son is greater than any given law.

God's Law is engraved in that spirit. Jeremiah 31:33

The spirit of a son is a generous spirit because it is one spirit with Jesus. 1 Corinthians 6:17

When a son is brought under the Law, the spirit that is in him is undermined. By enforcing Old Testament laws on a born again Christian, one actually asserts that a spirit of a son is a rebellious spirit and needs to be brought under the Law. That is the reason the Law is being used to make people give.

If Malachi 3:10 was the means through which God would get money out of His children, then:

1. He has failed in creating a new spirit in them. Ezekiel 11:19

2. He did not write His Law in their hearts.
Jeremiah 31:33

3. The only way for us to obey the Father would be through fear, repercussion, punishment, and curses.

Do you believe that?

By the way, if we are still under the law of tithing, why aren't churches following the biblical patterns of tithing? These are:

1. To support the priests and Levites – church ministers and workers. Numbers 18:21

2. To bring a portion of it to the church for a communal meal with the Lord. Deuteronomy 14:23-26

3. To support aliens, fatherless, and widows who dwelt in the land of Israel. Deuteronomy 14:28-29

4. Give a tenth of the people's tithe to the Lord's work. Numbers 18:26

Of the above commands on tithing, churches only practice point 1.

Wouldn't they also be under the curse themselves, since they are not fully following the tithing commands?

4

NEW TESTAMENT GIVING

Let's take a look at what God has created in this New Creation Man, and how generous this man truly is. Let's see if this man, under the new covenant, has a greater spirit of giving than the man under the old covenant.

First of all, remember that the New Testament, or the new covenant, is based upon a better covenant and better promises. The Bible says:

But now He has obtained a more excellent ministry, inasmuch as He is also Mediator of a better covenant, which was established on better promises. **Hebrews 8:6**

So, we have a better covenant with better promises.

The majority of church people do not know that there is a huge gap between the old and the new covenant. With all due respect, I doubt if most of our Bible teachers and ministers know the difference between these two covenants.

The teachings that we hear today in our churches are a mixture of the old and the new covenants. As a matter of fact, many of the doctrines of today's church are based upon the old covenant. The reason could be that the Protestant movements are just an upgraded version of the Catholic Church, and the Catholic doctrine is mainly based on works (the Law).

Thus, the Church, as far as I perceive, has never had a solid foundation in the new covenant doctrines.

A Covenant of Grace

To understand the new covenant, we need to start reading from the book of Romans, the first doctrinal book of the New Testament.

In regard to the new covenant, no other apostle had a greater revelation than the Apostle Paul, the man who wrote two thirds of the New Testament. Therefore, Paul's Epistles are of great importance to us in understanding the new covenant.

Somehow, Paul saw this more clearly than Peter, even though Peter walked with the Lord for three and a half years and was considered the pillar of the church in Jerusalem.

I am a firm believer that God does not give us His revelation beyond the level of our comprehension or perception. If He did, we would add our own thoughts to His Word. We would mix it with our cultures, thinking, and philosophies. It would be a half and half concoction – half of it would be truth, and the other half would be our sense knowledge.

This is why people, mainly preachers, can listen to the message of Redemption and never respond to it. They will continue teaching the fallacies they have been teaching for years. Pride will hinder them in seeing and understanding the truth.

This happened to the Jewish leaders in the time of Jesus. They could not receive Jesus as their Messiah. Jesus did not appear to their senses as the Messiah. He looked too simple, weak – too ordinary; a friend of sinners. There was no glamour, no fireworks about Him. He did not look or act like most preachers of His time.

You see, the Law gives you control over people. If you are a teacher of the Law, you have authority over people. Religious control of the masses is known throughout human history. Jesus practiced authority without threatening the people through the Law, and that confused the religious leaders of His time. He walked only by one law – the law of Love.

A Christian leader who uses the Law to control his people does not understand the working of God's Grace. Notice what Paul tells the believers in Ephesus before he departs: *And now, brethren, I commend you to God, and to the word of his grace, which is able to build you up, and to give you an inheritance among all them which are sanctified.* **Acts 20:32 KJV**

He does not leave them with a bunch of commands – do this and don't do that – but with the Word of God's Grace.

You see, it is the Word of God that gives us Grace, builds us, and conforms us to His image.

This is what the church needs today – the truth of God's Word, the word of His Grace.

Did you know that Paul was committed to the Gospel of Grace?

And see, now I go bound in the spirit to Jerusalem, not knowing the things that will happen to me there, except that the Holy Spirit testifies in every city, saying that chains and tribulations await me. But none of these things move me; nor do I count my life dear to myself, so that I may finish my race with joy, and the ministry which I received from the

Lord Jesus, to testify to the gospel of the grace of God. Acts
20:22-24

Notice, it is not the Gospel of works, but rather, the
Gospel of Grace. If we understand this, we can
understand the New Testament.

Look at how Paul encourages the Corinthian church
in regard to giving:
*Moreover, brethren, we make known to you **the grace of
God bestowed on the churches of Macedonia:** that in a
great trial of affliction the abundance of their joy and their
deep poverty abounded in the riches of their liberality. For I
bear witness that according to their ability, yes, and beyond
their ability, they were freely willing, imploring us with
much urgency that we would receive the gift and the
fellowship of the ministering to the saints. And not only as
we had hoped, but they first gave themselves to the Lord, and
then to us by the will of God. So we urged Titus, that as he
had begun, so he would also complete this grace in you as
well. But as you abound in everything – in faith, in speech,
in knowledge, in all diligence, and in your love for us – see
that you abound in this grace also.* 2 Corinthians 8:1-7,
Emphasis added

Paul talks about how the giving of the churches in
Macedonia was based upon God's Grace. He
encourages the Corinthian church to give. How? He
tells them to abound in this Grace: *See that you abound
in this grace also.*

What Grace is he talking about? Giving. So, giving
is a work of God's Grace in us – *They first gave
themselves to the Lord, and then to us by the will of God.*

He does not say, "God will bless them, if they give."
He does not say, "They will be cursed, if they do

not give."

He mentions nothing about tithing, the first fruit, free will offerings, or anything that relates to the old covenant.

He talks about God's Grace.

Notice the following verse: *And God is **able to make all grace abound toward you**, that you, always having all sufficiency in all things, may have an abundance for every good work.* 2 Corinthians 9:8

Do you see it? It is all Grace.

This is why Paul was unpopular in his time. He was consecrated unto the Lordship of Jesus and His Gospel of Grace.

This is often the case with those who love the truth. They are unpopular and do not fit among their peers. They are square pegs that do not fit in most religious round holes.

But thank God for them; although few in number, they carry an incredible burden that feeds the souls of millions who love God and His truth. They are carriers of the truth and the mysteries of the Gospel.

Their capacity for the truth is unlimited. They understand more spiritual truths in one minute than the majority of religious people can understand in an entire lifetime. 1 Corinthians 2:15

Notice what the Scripture says in Ephesians 3:4-5 (NIV) concerning the revelation of God's truth:

In reading this, then, you will be able to understand my insight into the mystery of Christ, which was not made known to men in other generations as it has now been revealed by the Spirit to God's holy apostles and prophets.

You see, God reveals His mystery to His holy apostles and prophets. The word *holy* means consecrated, or separated unto. These are men and women consecrated unto the truth of God's Word – consecrated unto the Gospel of our God and Savior.

They get it.

They see it.

They love God with all their hearts.

They are God's apostles.

They oversee the truth. They watch over it.

They are carriers of God's burden.

They are God's prophets. They see the truth and proclaim it regardless of what the consequences may be.

The Mystery of Christ

In Ephesians, Paul speaks of the mystery of Christ.

Redemption is a mystery.

The Gospel is a mystery – the mystery of how God, through Christ, accomplished everything for us freely.

It is a mystery.

We know bits and pieces, but the fullness of it is hidden from our eyes.

A mystery is a hidden truth. It cannot be obtained by sense knowledge.

It comes only by revelation to those who have receptive and humble spirits. I know people who have sat under our teachings for years and still do not see the new covenant. They still teach the principles of the old covenant. I have always wondered why. They heard the same teaching that the others did, yet they did not understand it.

It was hidden from their eyes.

Do you want to know why?

It is because of traditions, denominational doctrines, pride, and unscriptural practices.

A Baptist man was so touched by reading my book, *Redemption, An Unknown Inheritance*, that he has been giving a copy of it to as many people as he possibly can. He has purchased hundreds of copies and has spread them everywhere. He gave a copy of it to his preacher friend and asked for his opinion. After his preacher friend read the book, he told him, "The book is scriptural, but it is not practical!" This came as a shock to my friend. He asked me, "If it is scriptural, shouldn't it be practical?"

That preacher's answer is the exact description of the modern church. There are so many practices and teachings in the church these days that are not based upon the new covenant. They are practiced and taught because they are commonly accepted – everyone is saying and doing it. But does that make it right? One and a half billion Muslims pray against God's Word five times every day. Should their prayer be accepted as the truth because there are many of them doing it?

How do we measure the truth, and what is our measuring rod?

Preachers' doctrines?

Denominational doctrines?

Today's fad?

Or is it God's Eternal Word?

If we do not love the truth, and if we do not stand for it, our capacity for it will be diminished – not by God – but by our own religious mindsets. Now, if we reject the truth once it is revealed to us, then we are in danger of being deceived and are led to believe in falsehood.

The New Covenant

What is the new covenant?

I think one of the keys to the new covenant is found in the Gospel of John.

For the law was given through Moses, but grace and truth came through Jesus Christ. John 1:17

As we have discussed earlier, the foundation of the new covenant is based upon *Grace* – it is the free gift of God.

Grace is God's provision with no regards to our works, deeds, or actions. Grace is God's Love in action.

God made it happen before we did a thing.

God did it all by Himself.

The provision is made for all mankind, every single soul. And the only way one can tap into that provision is by having simple faith in the works of Jesus, namely, His Death, Burial, and Resurrection.

If one believes, in his heart, what Jesus has done in His Death, Burial, and Resurrection, and confesses with his mouth the Lordship of Jesus over his life, he will receive the free gift of God. Romans 10:9-10

Grace

Let's look at what the Scripture says concerning Grace:

Now when a man works, his wages are not credited to him as a gift, but as an obligation. However, to the man who does not work but trusts God who justifies the wicked, his faith is credited as righteousness. Romans 4:4-5 NIV

Also notice Romans 11:6: *And if by grace, then it is no longer by works; if it were, grace is no longer grace.*

Here we clearly see the difference between Grace and works.

You see, if you come to work for me, at the end of the day I will hand you a check for the service you have rendered. When I hand you the check, I cannot say that I am blessing you. Your pay was not a gift; it was the wages for your labor. Had you not worked and you still received a check, then it would have been considered a gift, a blessing.

Here is one other very important point: when you work, you do not need to have faith to receive your paycheck.

Faith is only appropriate when you do not work and yet still receive a paycheck. Thus, where work is involved, faith has no place.

Faith is only needed where Grace is applied.

Thus,

Grace needs faith,
The Law needs works.

This principle is a master key for understanding the new covenant.

Many people confuse the works of the Law with the works that come after faith.

The works that James talks about in James 2:14-26 are not the works of the Law. They are the works of faith – the types of works that are the product of our God-given faith.

Love, patience, peace, joy, forgiveness, giving, etc. – these are faith's outcomes.

The works prior to Jesus were the works of the Law. They were not produced in us by the faith of God, but rather an external force (the Law) made us perform them.

The works of the Law needed obedience, not faith.

Nowhere in the Old Testament was a Jew ever demanded to have faith in order to obey the Law. They had to be willing and obedient.

If you are willing and obedient, you shall eat the good of the land. Isaiah 1:19

The relation between Grace and faith is made clear to us in the following scripture:

For by grace you have been saved through faith, and that not of yourselves; it is the gift of God. Ephesians 2:8

Here we clearly understand that what God has done for us is all by His Grace and not by our works.

As a matter of fact, all of the blessings that we receive under the new covenant are because of His Grace. They are all free gifts of God.

This is the foundation of the new covenant.

Blessed be the God and Father of our Lord Jesus Christ, who has blessed us with every spiritual blessing in the heavenly places in Christ. Ephesians 1:3

When did He bless us? When we gave tithe? When we gave offerings?

No. A thousand times NO.

Then when?

When He loved us and paid the price for us through His Death, Burial, and Resurrection.

You are blessed with every spiritual blessing that is in the heavenly places.

Every single one of them.

It is all because of Jesus.

He blessed you with all blessings before you were even born. Your simple faith in the Lordship of Jesus has made them all available to you.

Wow! Go ahead and shout.

Get up and shake yourself from all the works of religion.

Say it out loud: "I am blessed because of Jesus." And keep saying it until it registers in every fiber of your being.

MALACHI AND THE NEW BIRTH

I would like to give you several reasons why Malachi 3 does not apply to a believer in the New Testament.

1. Reason One: The New Birth

One of the reasons we are no longer under the Law is because of our born again spirit.

The new creation in Christ is the greatest of all God's creations. As a matter of fact, this creation is so awesome that God could not make it any greater. The new creation is the crown of all of God's creations; God duplicated Himself in man through Jesus Christ. *Therefore, if anyone is in Christ, he is a new creation; old things have passed away; behold, all things have become new.* 2 Corinthians 5:17

This new birth is God birthing Himself in us. John tells us, *He came to His own, and His own did not receive Him. But as many as received Him, to them He gave the right to become children of God, to those who believe in His name: who were born, not of blood, nor of the will of the flesh, nor of the will of man, but of God.* John 1:11-13

The new creation is born of God.

That is you and I.

We are born of God – born from above.

John testifies of this truth again in his Epistle: *You*

are of God, little children, and have overcome them, because He who is in you is greater than he who is in the world. 1 John 4:4

Pay careful attention to the language of the Son of God when He speaks of this new creation. *For it was fitting for Him, for whom are all things and by whom are all things, in bringing many sons to glory, to make the captain of their salvation perfect through sufferings. For both He who sanctifies and those who are being sanctified are all of one, for which reason He is not ashamed to call them brethren.* Hebrews 2:10-11

Notice this truth: *are all of one.*

Our make-up is the same; the same nature, the same mind, the same purpose, the same inheritance, the same Father.

Wow, do you see it?

See how the Father talks about us:

And we know that all things work together for good to those who love God, to those who are the called according to His purpose. For whom He foreknew, He also predestined to be conformed to the image of His Son, that He might be the firstborn among many brethren. Romans 8:28-29

The moment you become a born again believer, you become one spirit with Jesus. 1 Corinthians 6:17

The Father would not have allowed you to be mixed with His Holy Son if you were not of the same spirit and the same nature as He.

He made you one with Him.

You can declare just like the Lord Jesus did, *I and My Father are one.* John 10:30

Can our hearts handle all of this goodness?

Religion has dressed us in servant clothing.

Modern preachers have put on us what the Jews wore under the Law– the servant's garment. Actually, their teachings indicate that the people under the old covenant were more blessed than the people under the new covenant.

It is simply raw ignorance.

These preachers are fascinated with the Old Testament saints and stories. Most of their preachings are based on the Old Testament because they know very little about the new covenant.

They still preach on Goliath and how David slew him. They still talk about Joshua's, Elijah's, and Elisha's anointing.

These modern teachings on anointing have crippled the body of Christ from a sonship position. I encourage you to read my book, *The Glory of Sonship*, to understand how far church philosophers have taken us away from our Father.

In our modern churches, Christians fill the altars to sense a touch from God. This type of feeling gives them an assurance of salvation.

They are babes in Christ. They need a touch – an anointing – in order to feel loved. They desire man's anointing, not knowing that they already have an anointing from above. 1 John 2:20

They crowd the altars of the churches where there is a so-called *revival*, confessing the sins they confessed in the last revival meeting. They have no knowledge of who they are and what Jesus has made them to be. They are bound by their senses and lusts. They are like little toddlers running to and fro in search of love. They need some action in their lives – something that can appeal to their senses.

They are a liability in the Body of Christ.

I cannot blame them. They have not been taught the truth.

They lack the knowledge of God's power in their lives. They are actually searching for something that is already in their possession.

*And what the transcendent greatness of His **power in us** believers as seen in the working of His infinite might. When He displayed it in Christ by raising Him from the dead and seating Him at His own right hand in the heavenly realms.* Ephesians 1:19-20, Wey, Emphasis added

Where is the power that raised Jesus from the dead? Not in some preacher's anointed hand.

Not in some revival service.

It is *in* you.

Every single believer possesses the same anointing that Jesus had, or else John 14:12 would be a lie. *Most assuredly, I say to you, he who believes in Me, the works that I do he will do also; and greater works than these he will do, because I go to My Father.*

Just because you do not use that anointing, just because you do not feel it, does not mean you do not possess it.

Elisha's anointing? No.

God works more miracles by His Grace in one hour of our broadcast in the Middle East than Elisha did in his entire lifetime. Do you know how many blind, deaf, crippled, cancerous, and diseased people have been healed through our broadcasts these past few years? The numbers are staggering. Elisha could only have dreamed about this. I think it is even beyond what he could have imagined.

Why would I want to have his anointing? He did only twelve miracles in his entire life.

Why would you want some preacher's anointing when you can freely have the perfect anointing of the Son of God?

2. Reason Two: United with Christ

The second reason why we are no longer under the Law is because God, through the new birth, places us in the same category of a spirit being as He himself. 1 John 4:4

We are born of God. John 1:13

We are one spirit with Him. 1 Corinthians 6:17

The same Holy Spirit that was in Jesus is in you – in the same measure.

God did not diminish the Holy Spirit when He came to live in you.

It is the same Spirit with the same capacity and the same mission.

But if the Spirit of Him who raised Jesus from the dead dwells in you... Romans 8:11

What does it mean that I am one spirit with Him?

It means that I am one with Him in His nature.

What is God's nature?

Love.

John tells us that God is Love. 1 John 4:8

Love is God's nature.

That same Love nature is in you and me. Romans 5:5

What does Love do?

Love gives.

God so loved the world that He gave... John 3:16
Love gives the best.
... He gave His only begotten Son... John 3:16
God's Love nature is a giving nature.
He gives the best He has because He loves.
Love did not give only a portion – but all.
Love does not just give ten percent – but all.

Look at the first church and how they gave. These
are the Jews, who used to tithe under the old covenant.
*Nor was there anyone among them who lacked; for all
who were possessors of lands or houses sold them, and
brought the proceeds of the things that were sold, and laid
them at the apostles' feet; and they distributed to each as
anyone had need.* Acts 4:34-35
How much did they give after they sold their
possessions?
A tithe?
The first fruit?
A small offering?
How much?
They gave all.
Do you remember how you were filled with so
much joy when you became a newly born Christian?
You were filled with joy and peace, which caused
you to give. You gave everything people asked you.
You became so loving, giving, and forgiving.
What had happened to you?
God's nature came into you and you acted out that
nature automatically.
No one forced you to give or to forgive.
It was there. It was in you. You wanted to forgive
the whole world. You could not wait until they opened

the doors of the church for you to get in. You testified constantly about Jesus. You wanted to win souls. You loved on everyone.

Remember?

Then you went to church and started hearing teachings about giving and doing this-and-that. They put all kinds of condemnation on you and killed the seed of joy and giving on the inside of you. They dragged you out under the Law and hung you there to dry.

I spoke with a woman about her experience as a born again Christian. She told me that she was miserable for eight years after her salvation.

I asked her, "Why?"

"For eight years I thought that I had to do something for God to love me" she responded.

Isn't it amazing what the church's philosophy has done to people?

Most Christians today give because they are condemned. They give out of obligation and not out of love and joy.

We have not taught them Love.

We have taught them trade: *give and it shall be given back to you.*

If you give and expect it to be returned to you, you have not given. You have made a trade.

Love gives.

We have not taught them the new birth.

They do not know that they are sons of God by faith. Galatians 3:26

We have taught them the Law: *If you give, God will*

bless you.

We have made a loving God into a businessman – a taskmaster.

We have taught them condemnation.

Have you ever received the blessings that the preachers promised you?

You could not have.

If God blessed you because of your giving, then there would be no lack in any church that preaches sowing and reaping – everyone would be blessed thirty-fold, sixty-fold, and one hundred-fold.

If God blessed you because of your giving, then how would He clarify the following verse?

*For you know the grace of our Lord Jesus Christ, that though He was rich, yet for your sakes He became poor, **that you through His poverty** might become rich.* 2 Corinthians 8:9, **Emphasis added**

If God blesses us because of our giving, then what happened to Jesus becoming poor for our sakes?

Don't you dare say that this verse is talking about spiritual poverty. Read the entire chapter; Paul is talking about financial support of the saints in Macedonia.

God would have to disregard the works of Jesus in order to repay you because of your works. This almost borders on blasphemy.

Every single time you gave money and had joy, it was because you were moved by love and compassion.

Love is the motivation for our giving. This is why God loves a cheerful giver.

Tithe was an obligation under the old covenant. If people disobeyed, they would be cursed. Malachi 3:8-10

The very fact that Paul encourages the Corinthians to give cheerfully and not out of obligation should tell us that tithing does not belong to the new covenant. Read carefully what Paul says in 2 Corinthians 9:7:

So let each one give as he purposes in his heart, not grudgingly or of necessity; for God loves a cheerful giver.

Notice: *according to what he purposes in his heart....*

That cannot be a tithe because a tithe is a set amount.

The word *purpose* in the above verse means decision. The New International Version reads, *Each man should give what he has decided in his heart to give.* Tithe is a set amount for each person. Tithe is not decided, but rather, it is calculated.

If *you* are told to decide the amount, then it cannot be a tithe.

If tithing was under the new covenant, then Paul teaches against it in this verse, for what I purpose in my heart is different from what you purpose in your heart.

In tithing, I have no choice. The amount is fixed – ten percent of all that I earn, make, or grow.

Also notice: *not grudgingly, or of necessity...* The word *necessity* means out of obligation.

Tithe was an obligation.

In these two great chapters on giving, 2 Corinthians 8 and 9, Paul does not mention, not one time, the words tithe or tithing.

3. Reason Three: Love Is A Greater Force

The third reason why we should not, or cannot, operate under the Law is because Love has a greater outcome than the Law. Its result is greater.

In the Acts of the Apostles, we read about the type of giving that belongs to the new covenant:

Then those who gladly received his word were baptized; and that day about three thousand souls were added to them. And they continued steadfastly in the apostles' doctrine and fellowship, in the breaking of bread, and in prayers. Then fear came upon every soul, and many wonders and signs were done through the apostles. Now all who believed were together, and had all things in common, and sold their possessions and goods, and divided them among all, as anyone had need.

So continuing daily with one accord in the temple, and breaking bread from house to house, they ate their food with gladness and simplicity of heart, praising God and having favor with all the people. And the Lord added to the church daily those who were being saved. Acts 2:41-47

Notice: *...and sold their possessions and goods, and divided them to all men, as every man had need.*

They did not give only ten percent. They gave all. That is a greater result than tithing.

That is the giving of Love.

That is new covenant giving.

That is a selfless giving spirit. It is the way God gave; He gave His best, and He gave it freely. Romans 8:32

It is the type of giving that makes the heart of our Father joyful.

There were no needs amongst anyone in the church in Jerusalem.

This is God's plan for the church. God wants us to take care of His church, His Body, and His Gospel.

Someone may ask, "Are we to ask people to sell their possession and bring it to church?"

No.

We cannot; that would be the Law.

Remember, the Law demands works and Grace demands faith.

The new creation spirit in believers will lead them to give the best they have. Love is a greater force.

There are people who give most of their income to the work of the Lord. I know a man who gave 90% of his income to God's work. My son, Jonathan, gave 70% of his income one year. At times, I give more than 50% of my own personal income and over 20% of our family income. I am not, by any means, talking about our giving. It is all God's Grace. I am just trying to show you what happens when we operate in Love.

Last year my son, Jonathan, a high school student, pledged one thousand dollars during our fund raising banquette for our Nejat TV network. He worked as a video editor part-time at Nejat making $9 an hour at that time. He had to work a lot to make $1000. One day he fulfilled half of his pledge. He then told me, "Dad, I want to double my pledge every year." Who told him to give like that? I never promised him any blessings in return. My daughter gives 20% of her income to Nejat TV. I did not know about it until a few weeks ago. What caused these children to give this way?

God's nature in them.

God's Love in them.

Love gives.

You teach people who they are in Christ and what God has done for them, and they will give all they have for Him.

On the other hand, put people under the Law and they will become greedy. You have to pull a lot of tricks out of your hat to get them to give. And that is what is taking place in Christian ministries and churches today.

I have yet to see a man bound by the Law being generous.

It is the revelation of the divine Love in you that causes you to give all that you possess.

I personally know of so many believers in Iran who have sacrificed all they have for their faith in Jesus. Under the Islamic regime of the Ayatollahs, they have lost family members, houses, belongings, positions, and jobs. Some have even been tortured and have lost their loved ones in the Islamic prisons. What about them? What blessings do they receive?

Every time a preacher forces people to tithe, he breaks a great part of a believer's spirit toward God.

It is like telling my children that they have to wash dishes everyday in order to eat, and if they do not wash dishes then I will not feed them!

What kind of Father would that make me? What would happen to my relationship with my children if I were to treat them like that?

Now, I could demand it from my servant. Wash a dish a day, and in return, I give you a meal a day. It would be appropriate to make him work for his wages. That is fair. We have an agreement, a covenant. If he keeps his end of the deal, I will keep mine.

But this kind of agreement does not apply to my son. Everything I have is his automatically. Even if he does not do a blessed thing for me, it is still his. Have you ever noticed that the voice that cried out from heaven, *This is My Beloved Son, in whom I am well pleased,* did so before Jesus did a single miracle, or a single notable act?

God was not pleased with Jesus because He did some great works, but because He was Jesus, God's beloved Son.

I loved my children the day they were born.

I would do anything for them just because they are mine.

When my kids were little, I had to pad my entire house because of them. I changed my furniture and padded the edges of all the walls. My house turned ugly. My house became theirs and to their liking. Why? It is simply because they were my children and I loved them. Not because of what they did. On the contrary, they did nothing that benefited me.

I love my children more than my own life because they are my children. They are my flesh and blood. Do you think my love for my children is greater than God's love for His?

Isn't that what Jesus said?

All things that the Father has are mine. John 16:15

Was that because He did something for God and in return God blessed Him with everything?

A million times NO.

Did you know that we have the same Father as the Lord Jesus, and that we stand in the same relationship to Him as Jesus does?

We have the same privileges and the same love. *I in them, and You in Me; that they may be made perfect in one, and that the world may know that You have sent Me, and have loved them as You have loved Me.* John 17:23

We have the same partnership: *So Jesus said to them again, "Peace to you! As the Father has sent Me, I also send you.* John 20:21

We have the same inheritance, ...*and if children, then heirs — heirs of God and joint heirs with Christ, if indeed we suffer with Him, that we may also be glorified together.*
Romans 8:17

We have the same family and the same Father: *I am ascending to My Father and your Father.* John 20:17

May God forgive us for what we have done to members of the Father's family.

We have treated them like servants.

We have pushed them back into the slavery of the Law.

We have made them become suspicious of God's love.

No wonder preachers are constantly begging and threatening God's people. They have taught God's sons and daughters that they are servants, yet they expect them to act like sons and daughters.

How is that possible?

Giving is Loving the Gospel

Giving is loving. *God so loved the world that He gave His only begotten Son...* John 3:16

Love gives.

Love makes sacrifices.

Giving is an attitude of the heart.

Giving indicates that I am not selfish.

Giving shows that I am walking in Love.

When I walk in Love, I walk in God – for God is Love. 1 John 4:8

The person who gives is protecting something he

loves, something dear to him.

We give because we love the Gospel. We want to protect and spread the Gospel of our God. We know the result of the preaching of the Gospel. We know what happens when people hear the Word of God – the faith of God arises in their hearts and changes them forever. That is dear to us. We want to see lives changed. We want to see people who are bound by alcohol, drugs, sex, and all kinds of mess to be set free. That is precious to us. We want to see them get saved and delivered.

Our giving prepares the path for the Gospel. There will be no lack and no hurdles for the preachers of the Gospel.

It costs money to preach the Gospel. We know that. The Gospel is free to those who hear it, but it costs to those who love it.

The Gospel is ours. Paul says, …*according to my gospel.* Romans 2:16

God gave the Gospel to us.

He entrusted it to our care.

Look at 2 Corinthians: *Now all things are of God, who has reconciled us to Himself through Jesus Christ, and has given us the ministry of reconciliation, that is, that God was in Christ reconciling the world to Himself, not imputing their trespasses to them, and has committed to us the word of reconciliation.* 2 Corinthians 5:18-19

Notice verse 18: …*has given to us **the ministry** of reconciliation,* and in the next verse he tells us that God *has committed to us **the word** of reconciliation.* Emphasis added

We have both the *word* and the *ministry* of reconciliation.

In our ministry we have many testimonies where

the Lord Himself, or one of His angels, has appeared to people through either a dream or a vision. In either case, people were told to tune in to our TV channel, or to go to our crusade to hear the Word of God from us.

Once I was in the State of Bihar in India for an open-air crusade. The Lord appeared to a Hindu woman in her house. Actually, she saw Him walking in through the wall. He told her who He was and then told her to come to our crusade to hear the Word of God. She looked everywhere in that town trying to locate the crusade ground. She found it, came, and accepted Jesus as her only Lord and Savior.

In none of these cases was the Gospel preached by the angel or the Lord Himself. They told people to hear it from us.

It is simply because God gave us the *ministry* and the *word* of *reconciliation*.

It is our responsibility to bring people to Him.

We have the stewardship of the Gospel.

We carry the burden.

We must preach and proclaim it.

The world will walk in absolute darkness if we refuse to proclaim the Gospel.

Therefore, we must support the Gospel. We give because we love the souls of men. We make sacrifices for the sake of the Gospel.

6

INTERPRETING SCRIPTURES IN THE LIGHT OF OUR REDEMPTION

The modern interpretation of *give and it shall be given to you* is selfish.

It is based on man's selfish fallen nature and not on God's loving nature. Preachers nurture the fallen nature by promising people a multiplication return.

As we discussed earlier, Luke 6:38 neither speaks of money nor claims that God will give back to us what we have sown. It just simply tells us how we should conduct ourselves towards others. For the way we treat others, we will be treated in like manner.

Luke 6:38 is a natural law operating in the realm of senses. If we treat people kindly, they will, in turn, treat us kindly – regardless of whether or not they are believers in Christ.

If you buy dinner for someone, he will buy you a dinner.

Now, when we interpret the Scripture, we have to interpret it in accordance to the covenant in which the Scripture was given. The Scripture is given in accordance to God's plan and God's purposes.

We cannot and should not mix the Old Testament concepts with those of the New Testament. For instance, Paul tells us that we should speak to one another in Psalms, ...*speaking to one another in psalms and hymns and spiritual songs, singing and making melody in your heart to the Lord.* Ephesians 5:19

Now, there are many scriptures in the book of Psalms where David wishes death and destruction upon his enemies. Here are just a few:

*Strike all my **enemies** on the jaw; break the teeth of the wicked.* Psalm 3:7 NIV, Emphasis added

*All my **enemies** will be ashamed and dismayed; they will turn back in sudden disgrace.* Psalm 6:10 NIV, Emphasis added

*My **enemies** turn back; they stumble and perish before you.* Psalm 9:3 NIV, Emphasis added

*I pursued my **enemies** and overtook them; I did not turn back till they were destroyed.* Psalm 18:37 NIV, Emphasis added

The question is, can you meditate on these scriptures and claim them?

Paul definitely does not mean for us to make melody and hymns out of the above Psalms of David, does he?

Why not?

Simply because what David claims in these scriptures contradict the essence of the New Testament, which is based upon the Grace and the Love of our Lord Jesus. Under the new covenant we are to pray for those who persecute us. Are we not?

In like manner, we cannot mix the Old and the New Testaments' concepts of giving.

Now, let us look at the following scripture and try to interpret it according to the New Testament:

But this I say: He who sows sparingly will also reap sparingly, and he who sows bountifully will also reap

bountifully. 2 Corinthians 9:6

Almost every preacher, teacher, and pastor that I have heard quote this scripture interpret it as following:

"If we sow little money, we will reap little money. If we sow a lot of money, we will reap a lot of money."

We need to learn the principle of biblical interpretation. The Scripture is given in the framework of the covenant. Just like Jesus said, *And no one puts new wine into old wineskins; or else the new wine will burst the wineskins and be spilled, and the wineskins will be ruined.* Luke 5:37

Using the above principle, I can instantly recognize the wrongful interpretation of 2 Corinthians 9:6 as I have heard it.

Let me explain.

Before we interpret this scripture, we need to know its context.

The entire two chapters of 2 Corinthians 8 and 9 are about the Corinthians raising funds for the needs of the churches in Macedonia. So when we interpret 2 Corinthians 9:6, we must take into consideration the context of chapters 8 and 9. For in these two chapters, Paul is talking about the same subject.

When Paul wrote these letters, they were not written in chapters and verses. Just like when you write a letter to a friend, you do not divide it into chapters and verses. The chapters and verses were added later during the canonizations of the Bible for a better means of reference.

Also, concepts within the same context cannot contradict one another. In verse 6 Paul tells the Corinthians that if they sow bountifully, they will reap bountifully. Now, we know that the word *sow* here is referring to the Corinthians supporting the needs of the believers in Macedonia. But what does the word *reap* mean? The preachers tell us if we sow little money, we will reap little money, and if we sow a lot of money, we will reap a lot of money.

If the reaping in the above scripture means money, then we would have several major contradictions in chapters 8 and 9 of 2 Corinthians.

If the motivation of the giving by the Corinthians was getting more in return, then what do the following verses mean?

In verse 1 Paul says, *For as touching the ministering to the saints, it is superfluous for me to write to you.* 2 Corinthians 9:1

Here we understand that Paul is doing this fundraising for the needs of the saints in Macedonia.

So, Paul is talking about ministering to the needs of the saints in Macedonia – not growing the finances of the Corinthians.

In verse 5 Paul speaks against covetousness. *Therefore I thought it necessary to exhort the brethren, that they would go before unto you, and make up beforehand your bounty, whereof ye had notice before, that the same might be ready, as a matter of bounty, and not as* of *covetousness.* 2 Corinthians 9:5 KJV

If I give in order to get back, and more of it, that would be called covetousness, wouldn't it?

Then what are Corinthians reaping bountifully if it is not money? Notice the following verses: *For the administration of this service not only supplies the needs of the saints, but also is abounding through many thanksgivings to God, while, through the proof of this ministry, they glorify God for the obedience of your confession to the gospel of Christ, and for your liberal sharing with them and all men, and by their prayer for you, who long for you because of the exceeding grace of God in you.* 2 Corinthians 9:12-14

Read verse 12: *...supplies the needs of the saints, but also is abounding through many thanksgivings unto God...*

Also notice verse 8: *And God is able to make all grace abound toward you; that ye, always having all sufficiency in all things, may* **abound to every good work.** 2 Corinthians 9:8 KJV, Emphasis added

The reaping bountifully of which Paul is talking is *the good work*, supplying the needs of God's people. That is a good work.

For instance, let's say that it takes $1 to save a soul. If I give $10, ten souls will be saved. Now, how many souls would be saved if I were to give $100? One hundred souls.

Do you see it? The more I give, the more souls are saved.

He who sows sparingly will reap (the result of that sowing) sparingly.

Did you also notice verse 8? *God is able to make all* **grace** *abound towards you, that you...*

It is God's Grace that makes you abound, not your giving. Paul does not say, "If you give more, God will give you more money so that you may be blessed."

That is foolishness and greed.

Giving is a stewardship.

It is called *giving* and not *getting back*.

Stewardship

God is the author and sole possessor of all that is on the earth, in heaven above, and all that is in the ocean.

The earth is the LORD's, and all its fullness, the world and those who dwell therein. Psalm 24:1

For every beast of the forest is Mine, and the cattle on a thousand hills. Psalm 50:10

"The silver is Mine, and the gold is Mine," says the LORD of hosts. Haggai 2:8

The majority of people, including Christians, do not believe these scriptures. Christians may read them and acknowledge that God is the sole possessor of all things, but in reality they do not practice it. They consent to it, but they are not convicted in their hearts.

David had an understanding of this matter when he gave several trillion dollars in gold and silver in offerings for the building of God's temple. 1 Chronicles 28-29

Pay attention to what he declares after he gave the world's greatest offering ever given by an earthly man:

But who am I, and who are my people, that we should be able to offer so willingly as this? For all things come from You, and of Your own we have given You. 1 Chronicles 29:14

David recognized that what he had given was from God. And since it all belonged to God, David was not giving it; he was just simply returning it to God.

That is a mindset of a faithful steward.

Let me explain what a steward is.

Let's say that I owned a pomegranate orchard and had lent it to you free of charge to use the fruit for the needs of your family and friends. Then one day I asked you to deliver some of the fruit to my servants for their needs as well. How much of the fruit of that orchard belongs to me – one half, one third, or all?

I would say all.

I did not tell you how much to give; I left it to your generosity. Since I was extremely generous toward you, I was hoping you would learn from me and also be generous toward my servants.

What should I do if you were to give only one pound of the fruit to my servants? You reaped one thousand pounds, but only gave one pound away.

If I had a written contract with you and had asked you to deliver a certain amount yet you did not, I could have taken the orchard away from you. But since I had no contract with you and left it entirely to your generosity, then I could not demand you to be generous.

Here is my conclusion: Had you given away a lot of the fruit, then I would say you have an understanding of what I have done for you. If you had done the opposite and had given only a few pieces of fruit to my servants, then I would conclude that you are a proud person and have taken possession of what does not belong to you. You are an unfaithful, proud, and ignorant steward.

I have noticed the people who are very generous have the following characteristics in common:

- They do not think they deserve the wealth that has been given to them.
- They are humble.
- They love God.
- They love what their giving does for people.
- They are selfless.
- They are simple.

- They do not think they earned it, but rather they are fortunate.

THE NATURE OF A SON

A Christian is a Christ-like being. The Bible declares, *Therefore, if anyone is in Christ, he is a new creation; old things have passed away; behold, all things have become new.* 2 Corinthians 5:17

Another translation says *He is a new species of being.* This new creation is born of God. John 1:13

He is partaker of the divine nature. 2 Peter 1:3

God's life is in this new creation. John 5:24

John tells us, *He who has the Son has life; he who does not have the Son of God does not have life.* 1 John 5:12

Jesus said, *Most assuredly, I say to you, he who hears My word and believes in Him who sent Me has everlasting life, and shall not come into judgment, but has passed from death into life.* John 5:24

The term *everlasting life* is translated from the Greek word *Zoe.* It means God's life, that which is in the Father God.

A believer possesses the very life of God.

We have passed from death, the domain of satan, to life, the domain of God.

We are no longer under the authority of satan and death. Colossians 1:13

Sin and death no longer have dominion over us. Romans 6:14

That old nature, which was ruled by satan, has been

crucified with Christ. Romans 8:3

Man lived in the domain and realm of spiritual death until Jesus was crucified on the cross,
For He made Him who knew no sin to be sin for us, that we might become the righteousness of God in Him.
2 Corinthians 5:21

Jesus became what you and I were – darkness.
Ephesians 5:8

We were crucified with Him. Galatians 2:20

We no longer live. He lives in us. Galatians 2:20

His Love is in us. Romans 5:5

The life of God that was in Him is now in us. John 5:24

His giving is in us.

His compassion for souls is in us.

Christ with all His fullness lives in us.

I have been crucified with Christ; it is no longer I who live, but Christ lives in me; and the life which I now live in the flesh I live by faith in the Son of God, who loved me and gave Himself for me. Galatians 2:20

We are no longer in subjection to selfishness and greed.

The old stingy nature, which was self seeking and selfish, was crucified on the cross.

A New Man has risen who is made in the very likeness of the Son of God.

This new nature is a Love nature, *...because the love of God has been poured out in our hearts by the Holy Spirit...* Romans 5:5

This Love nature gives.

This Love nature forgives.

It is God Himself operating in us.

It would be an insult to His Majesty to bind this

84

New Man under the Law.

Notice what Paul says in Galatians 2:21: *I do not set aside the grace of God; for if righteousness comes through the law, then Christ died in vain.*

If I receive blessings through tithing, then Jesus became poor in vain. *For you know the grace of our Lord Jesus Christ, that though He was rich, yet for your sakes He became poor, that you through His poverty might become rich.* 2 Corinthians 8:9

The word rich here means *fully supplied.*

He became poor for your sake so that you may become fully supplied.

You receive your blessings through His poverty, not through your giving. It is through His works, not yours.

We are blessed with every spiritual blessing through Him. Ephesians 1:3

Tithe is an ordinance for servants.

Servants are not expected to take care of the Father's business – the sons are.

For you are all sons of God through faith in Christ Jesus. Galatians 3:26

A son should give more to the Father than a servant.

All that the Father has belongs to the son. Jesus said, *All things that the Father has are Mine.* John 16:15

If the son claims his Father's belongings, then the Father should do the same, even greater. So we could say, all that the Son has belongs to the Father. Isn't this what Paul says?

…whether Paul or Apollos or Cephas, or the world or life or death, or things present or things to come – all are yours. And you are Christ's, and Christ is God's. 1 Corinthians 3:22-23

Jesus claimed all that the Father has. And here we read that Christ is God's.

Wouldn't it be a sin for a son to say that only ten percent of what he has belongs to the Father?

All of what a son has belongs to the Father.

I believe this is why the church is in great financial bondage. This is why the world thinks of preachers as money mongers. This is why the church has never fully fulfilled the Great Commission. This is why Christians are constantly in need. They have followed the doctrines of men.

Organized religion has stripped the church of its rights and privileges. It has put a yoke of servanthood on us.

Instead of teaching us who we are in Christ and what we have, they have taught us who we are not and what we do not possess.

Future Tense Theology

It is said that only 3% to 6% of all Christians tithe. With all the condemnation that is put on the church, people still do not tithe. Why is it? It is simply because they are not taught the truth.

Pastors command their congregation to believe God for finances, yet they fail to do it themselves. They command their people to tithe, but their ministry, or church, fails to do so itself.

How many churches do you know that tithe? I only know of a few churches that give tithe to missions.

The tenses that religion uses in regard to God's

blessings are always in the future – "God *is going* to save your family member," "God *is going* to open a door to you," "God *is going* to cancel your debt," etc.

Notice all of these verbs are in the future tense. You know what that means – people do not know what Jesus has already accomplished through His Redemptive work.

They do not know that **He has [already]** blessed us with all spiritual blessings. Ephesians 1:3

They do not know that **His divine power has [already]** provided for us all things that we need for life and godliness. 2 Peter 1:3

They do not know that **He has [already]** delivered us from the power of darkness. Colossians 1:13

They do not know that, **He has [already]** redeemed us from the curse of the Law. Galatians 3:13

Notice the tenses of these blessings. They are all present perfect tenses. Present perfect means the action began sometime in the past and the result of it is still in operation today.

It is all done.

Jesus is seated at the right hand of God.

It is all finished.

There is only one "going to do" left for Him – His return to take us home.

Every time someone says, "God is going to…" note what they say afterward and test it against the Word of God. Most likely, what they are promising you has already been done for you by Jesus' Redemptive work.

Be extra careful when they say that you have to give in order to get something from God.

They tell us that if we give, God *is going to* bless us. We have developed a mentality that we have to buy our way into God's blessing. We have made a loving God into a businessman. It is no wonder that the church does not trust Him.

May God forgive our ignorance and foolishness.

Sons of God

Let's dwell on the new covenant.

Let's find out what Jesus has accomplished through His Death, Burial, and Resurrection.

Let's discover who we are in Him through His Redemption.

Let's find out more about this New Man that God has created in Christ Jesus.

Let's study the person and the life of the Son of God.

He left us an example of how to act as a son – for we are all sons of God by faith. Galatians 3:26

Read the Gospel of John and meditate on it as often as you can.

Look at Jesus, God's Son, our beloved older brother.

We belong to His family. Hebrews 2:11

We have the same Spirit that was in Him. Romans 8:11

We have the same nature. 2 Peter 1:3

We have the same mission. John 20:21

We have the same mind that He has. 1 Corinthians 2:16

We have the same Love in us that was in Him. Romans 5:5

We give because He first gave.

We love because He first loved us. 1 John 4:10-11

It is following the path that the Master walked on before us.

Hallelujah!

You are a giver because you are born of God. John 1:13
You have a generous spirit because He was rich and for your sake became poor. 2 Corinthians 8:9
You love Him and His Gospel because He first loved you. 1 John 4:10-11
God's Spirit dwells in you. Romans 8:11
That makes you a victor. 1 John 4:4
You are a giver because you love the souls of men.
You are a giver because it is more blessed to give. Acts 20:35
You are a giver because you are blessed. Ephesians 1:3
You are a giver because you are a lover. Romans 5:5
You are a son of God. Galatians 3:26

To God be the glory for His indescribable Grace and Love.

PARABLE OF TWO HOUSES

There are two different houses built by the same builder. The first house is an amazing house; it is glamorous, has many pictures, and has many adornments. The second house is simple and small, yet it has a glory about it that surpasses that of the first house.

The first house has enough space for only one family. The second, though small in size, can house the entire neighborhood.

The first has many rules for its residents. The second has only one rule.

The residents of the first house can only enjoy the benefits of the house *if* they obey the rules of the house. The residents of the second house, though, can enjoy the benefits *immediately* upon their arrival to the house. The only prerequisite to enjoy the benefits of the second house is to be a resident of it.

The foundation of the first house is made from a material called *The Law of Moses*. The foundation of the second house is a mysterious compound called *Grace*.

The material in the first house is expensive for the tenants, but inexpensive for the builder. Whereas the material known as *Grace,* of which the second house is made, is free for the tenants but extremely costly for the builder.

The builder named the first house *Old Plan,* and the second house *New Plan.*

Since the second house has many more benefits than the first house, the residents of the first house were invited to move to the second house.

They did not.

The builder eventually abandoned the first house. His intention for the first house was to build a temporary residential place. His goal from the beginning was to have everyone live in the second house.

The builder loves the residents of the first house. Although he has abandoned the house, he cares for the people who are still living in it. He hopes that the residents of the first house will eventually realize that they need to move to the new house. Actually, some of the residents have already moved and many are praying for the remaining residents.

The problem is that the residents of the first house are attached to all the ornaments and all the pictures that were placed in the first house. There were beautiful ornaments that made the residents of the first house feel special because no other houses had ever been built with such ornaments anywhere in the world. The builder, however, has created a greater beauty in the second house that causes great joy to all who live in it. He believes that the obvious joy and the love that is seen in the people of the second house will make the residents of the first house jealous enough to make them move to the second house.

We hope so, too.

Recently, there has developed a problem among the residents of the second house. The problem started when some of the leaders of the second house began visiting the first house. They expressed their friendliness by asking what the ornaments meant. They were fascinated by all the ornaments.

The leaders of the second house gradually became jealous of all the pictures and ornaments of the first house. They felt as though their house was too simple. Trying to make their house more beautiful, the people in the second house borrowed some of the pictures and ornaments from the first house. Some even dared to steal a portion of the foundation of the first house and mix it with the foundation of the second house. They reasoned that the *Law of Moses* foundation would last forever.

Thus, they defiled the foundation of the second house called *Grace*.

So now, there are ornaments and pictures in the second house.

It is of course forbidden to add ornaments or pictures to the second house. The builder is very upset with what some of the leaders of the second house have done. This has caused much confusion among the residents of the second house.

Some leaders have spoken publicly saying that the residents of the first house do not need to move to the second house at all. They reason that since the first house was built by the same builder, it is good enough for eternal residency. These leaders are known as *Dual Housers*.

Some argue that these *Dual Housers* have not read the manual of the second house. Still others believe that it is only a political move to gain fame, recognition, and even benefits.

They want to be popular in both houses. In any

case, there is major confusion in the second house.

Actually, the second house was built by the builder's son, a renowned contractor. He feels very hurt by the people who have committed this treacherous act, because these people have rejected him and his model home, which was designed to be a perfect house all by itself, without any pictures and ornaments.

Hopefully the leaders and their followers in the second house, who have caused all this confusion, will soon realize what they have done and repent of their misbehavior. Or else they will have no rewards for all their services rendered to both houses.

The *Dual Housers* are also known as *Lukewarms*, because they have meshed the old and the new foundations into one mixture.

It is interesting to note that the builder knew this would happen, so he dedicated a small group of inspectors, who love the builder and his son, to go to the second house and explain the foundation of the two houses.

So far there have only been a handful of solid inspectors willing to examine the blue prints and inform the people of the truth. Many were called to be an inspector for the builder's son, but they refused. They were happy with the way life had been going on for centuries in these two houses and did not want to ruffle any feathers.

The first great inspector was a man from Syria by the name of Saul of Tarsus, a great friend of the builder's son. He actually wrote the main part of the builder's manual on the second house. The second one was a man from Germany by the name of Martin

Luther. And the third one is from the United States by the name of E.W. Kenyon. Hopefully, more inspectors, of the same caliber as these men, will be sent out to the second house to inform people, since these men of old have all passed away.

LAST WORD

A Word to Pastors

The teaching of this book may have caused some concern to you in regard to how you should teach your people about giving. If you find this teaching to be in accordance with the truth of the Scripture and you are still a bit concerned about what to do, let me give you some encouraging words.

Your congregation's giving is mostly based on each individual's relationship to the Lord. If they love Him, they will give and sacrifice much. If they do not love God, no matter what you say to them it will not have great impact on their giving.

Currently, by God's Grace, I oversee about 100 churches throughout the world among the Persian-speaking people. I pastored my last English church, which I started in Tulsa, Oklahoma, for fourteen years. Several years before I resigned, I taught them rightfully about money and giving. You would be amazed to know how little I said about offerings and money during our services. Yet, the giving of the church did not change much. Those who did not give continued not to give. And those who loved God continued to give and gave beyond measure at times. I loved them all the same.

Giving is an issue of the heart. Jesus said, *For where your treasure is, there your heart will be also.* Matthew 6:21

The modern philosophers of the church have added so many gimmicks in order to get people to give. I understand that the bills have to be paid – such as building projects, staff salaries, TV broadcasts, and so many other things.

It seems as though the purity of our faith has been lost in the shuffle of things. We are more and more mechanical. It almost sounds like our goal is to meet the budget rather than maturing the saints of God.

The key has always been the same – Jesus. It is about Him and not our vision, ministry, building projects, or goals. There is so much talk about vision these days that it is not healthy. The focus must be on Him – His Love, His vision, His Church, etc.

All He is asking us to do is what He asked Peter, "Feed my flock." If we teach people who they are in Christ and what He has done for them, if we teach them the truth of God's Word, then they will be built up and will come into a rightful relationship with the Lord. Then they will do everything for Him.

They will give their best before you even ask them for it. We do not need to manipulate, use gimmicks, make promises, or do anything else to get them to give. God's nature in them will lead them to do what is right. Just keep telling them who Jesus is, what He has done, and who they have become in Him. I hope and pray that this book has been a blessing to you and that

you have been challenged in this area.
I pray that you may feed His flock.

In His Love,
Pastor Reza Safa

About the Author

Pastor Reza Safa was born into a Shi'ite Muslim family in the Middle East. He was a devout, practicing Shi'ite Muslim, observing the laws of Islam. He fasted during the month of Ramadan and prayed five times a day.

After his graduation from high school, Safa felt an emptiness nagging at him. The search for truth led him to leave his homeland and reside in the West. Safa finally settled as a student in Sweden, where he heard the message of the gospel for the first time in his life. Reading the Bible in his native language and experiencing the love of God through Christian friends, Safa decided to give Jesus a chance. After months of struggle and doubt, he finally gave his life to Jesus.

In 1990 Pastor Reza Safa founded The Harvesters World Outreach, a worldwide evangelistic and healing ministry. Since then he has held crusades and pastors conferences in over 50 countries. People from all religions, especially those from Muslim and Hindu backgrounds have turned to Christ in his crusades.

After a vision from the Lord and several years of prayer, Nejat TV was born and began airing Christian TV programming into the Middle East. (Nejat means *salvation* in the Farsi language.) In March 2003, regular broadcasts began four hours a week on a secular Persian television network based in California. A partnership with Trinity Broadcasting Network (TBN) was formed in 2006 and TBN Nejat TV, a full time satellite television network in the Farsi language was launched. The response was overwhelming. According to some research, three to five million Iranian Muslims have come to Christ as a result of these Christian broadcasts. Over ninety underground churches have been established in Iran. Satellite television is being aired in areas of the Middle East where no person has the means or possibility of reaching with the gospel of Jesus Christ. A door has been opened by God to preach the Gospel and no government or religious organization can close this door.

We would greatly appreciate your support and your prayers for this great outreach to Iran and the Middle East. If you would like to receive more information on TBN Nejat TV, please visit our website, ww.nejattv.org, or call our office at (805) 445-7744.

ALSO BY REZA SAFA

REDEMPTION

Redemption is the most important subject of the Bible. It is the entire work of God through our Lord Jesus Christ. Without a proper understanding of the Redemption of Jesus Christ, the church remains bound by the yoke of the law, human philosophy, and the doctrines of men.   **$ 10.00**

BLOOD OF THE SWORD, BLOOD OF THE CROSS

Biography. Here is the true story of the hunger and thirst of a fanatical Muslim for God. Reza Safa's search for the truth took him across three continents. His belief in Islam remained unshakable until the day he heard the truth about Jesus Christ and began to experience His love.   **$ 10.00**

THE COMING FALL OF ISLAM IN IRAN

In *The Coming Fall of Islam in Iran*, former Shi'ite Muslim Reza Safa brings an awareness and knowledge about the mind-set of the enemy. He also explains how in spite of religious persecution - indeed, at times because of it - Iranians are coming to the Lord in droves.   **$ 15.00**

INSIDE ISLAM

Author Reza Safa, a former Shiíite Muslim, exposes the spirit of Islam from an insider's point of view. Safa is well versed in the laws and history of Islam.   **$ 12.00**

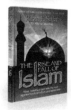

THE RISE AND FALL OF ISLAM

From inside Islam comes a prophetic message for America and how she must respond to terrorism and its radical religion. The Church must wake up to the spiritual time we are in and reach out for God's answers to the expanding force of Islam.   **$ 13.00**

P.O. Box 2030, Camarillo, CA 93011
Phone: 805-445-7744 • www.rezasafa.com

For more information on Reza Safa Ministries, please visit our website at: www.rezasafa.com or contact our office.

REZA SAFA MINISTRIES
P.O. BOX 2030
CAMARILLO, CA 93011

PHONE: (805) 445-7744
WWW.REZASAFA.COM